I0029957

Conscious Money

How to Master the Art of Sales by Mastering
Oneself

Bauer Doski, MA

Conscious Money: How to Master the Art of Sales by Mastering Oneself

Copyright © 2019 by Bauer Doski

All Rights Reserved. No part of this book or any of its contents may be reproduced, copied, modified, distributed, stored, transmitted in any form or by any means, or adapted without the prior written consent of the authors and publisher.

Publishing services provided by

Archangel Ink

This book represents my love for humanity and all those who are actively creating good for this abundant universe of ours.

Thank you to every family member—both blood and spiritual—who's instilled wisdom, consciousness, abundance, and strength in me. I'm forever blessed by your presence.

Your Free Resource

Before you begin reading, I have a free bonus to offer you!

In addition to the information already provided in this book, my team has created a Q&A pdf file to guide you through the chapters. I show how I've used the tools covered in this book to achieve success.

You can grab your free bonus right here: www.bauerdoski.com/ conscious- money-bonus

When you sign up, I'll notify you of any pending book or product releases and keep you updated on content that may be helpful for your journey to success. Oh, and you'll also be first in line for exclusive deals and future book giveaways!

Immediately after signing up, make sure to check your email for access to the bonus.

–Bauer

CONTENTS

PREFACE

You're probably wondering, *Is this a self-development book or a sales book?* But let me ask you: Aren't they the same? Isn't the art of finding, developing, believing in, and selling yourself to yourself exactly the same thing as finding, developing, believing in, and selling a product or service to yourself before you sell it to others?

Haha. Gotcha there!

Our society sometimes has a negative connotation about sales, even though it literally provides a livelihood for each and every one of us living in a free market society. Your profession doesn't need the word "sales" in it to be included. Consider that doctors sell improved health, a cure to a disorder, a procedure, medication, or a simple belief in the solutions handed to their patients. We're not just talking about a sleazy used car salesman. We are ALL salespeople to some degree. Some of us just have a fancy title to soften the idea of selling to our customers.

Let's face it, sales is sales across the board. Some of us sell products and services, while the rest of us sell ideas, beliefs, and even faith. No matter what industry we're talking about, each and every one of us is ultimately selling ourselves to our customers.

Combining sales with self-development allows these powerful fields to work together to create the person we hope to become.

Now, personally, I LOVE salespeople. Especially the ones who know how to master the art, those who know how to use it to get anything and everything they want in this beautiful universe of ours (with our morals top of mind, of course). You know the ones I'm talking about—those who sell a product and/or a service to a client in such a professional and seamless manner that the customer becomes so excited about the transaction, they don't even feel they're being sold to. By the time they're finished, they're happy to be buying the service!

That's what this book is about. I want you to become such an empowered, effective, enlivened salesperson that your customers are excited to do business with you. In this book, I will teach you the art of finding your inner power, that inner gold that you have yet to discover. With this skill under your belt, the world and all its riches can be yours.

I don't mean I will literally send money to your bank account. What I mean is that, with this book in your hands, you will discover where the money has been all along. I will help you realize where the potential and opportunities have been stored. I will help you find your true self and rake in a few coins while we're at it. So come along, and let's get you on the side where the grass really is greener.

INTRODUCTION

I didn't always love sales. I never said to myself, "Hey, I'm going to get really good at that one thing that most people are terrified of!" In fact, I was once scared to death of sales. I remember being a kid watching a jewelry salesperson as they approached my parents—how they would interact with them, the questions they'd ask, and the energy and vibe they'd give off. Their body language, tonality, and even word choice all determined how my parents, "the buyers," took the offer. Little did the salesperson know my parents were natural sales professionals.

My parents came from overseas. Growing up, living, and working in the Middle Eastern part of the world, my parents were taught to understand the importance of selling themselves more than any other product or service. If you'd asked either of them if they knew they were salespeople, they'd probably look at you funny. Funnier than the first time they looked at me when I told them I was going vegetarian. But we'll save that story for later.

My mom came from a very wealthy and educated family, and her siblings grew to become pharmacists, engineers, bankers, and professors; she became an agricultural engineer. After marrying my father and having us four kids, she decided to further her education and become both a mathematics and English professor. That would allow her to come home to her family after teaching her daily classes. In case you're not aware, this wasn't exactly in line with Middle Eastern cultural expectations. No matter; my mom sure knew what her values and abilities were, and whoever tried to tell her otherwise had something coming.

My dad, on the other hand, came from a poor village. I've heard him tell stories more than once about how he had to fast in order to save enough food for his siblings to eat. He was the youngest of twins and the baby of his family. His father passed away before he was born; as soon as he could walk, he was put to work. From being drafted into the Iraq and Kuwait war to finishing up school as the last remaining minutes of sunlight streaked through his family's single living room window, whatever challenge he met, he faced it head-on. My father finished his schooling and went on to become one of the few civil engineers in his village. He knew it didn't matter where he came from; that didn't determine where he was going.

My parents went about their lives working diligently on their dreams and having their children. Years into their marriage, after my mother made the career change, my father started working at an engineering gig with a group of American engineers. However, it wasn't long after that Mr. Hussein threatened engineers working with any non-Middle Easterner. So my parents fled, eventually finding their way to America and selling a few of their properties and businesses along the way.

My dad, being the true hustler that he was, landed his first engineering job on his third day in America at IBM. From there, he picked up a second job just one week later as a mechanic at a local car dealership. My mother, on the other hand, started teaching in a local elementary school, where most of us kids attended. On the side, she sold phone cards to any foreigner with family back in their hometown (that number was very large, especially in the less affluent neighborhoods that most foreigners resided in at the time). Despite each parent working two jobs and caring for four children between the ages of five and ten, they continued their education and attended a local community college to brush up on their English skills. They had a vision and knew that in order to achieve it, they had to fully understand and clearly speak the native language.

Now, you might think being sixty and sixty-four years old would stop them. I beg to differ! To this day, my parents are at the top of their game. They decided to grow their real estate portfolio and invest in properties here in the States. It wasn't long after they started that their holdings grew from one piece of property to over a few dozen. They grew their real estate internationally to a degree they'd never dreamed of. From residential apartment complexes to commercial buildings, they sure knew what they were doing. Ever heard that foreigners are great workers? Haha! That was my family to a T. Ever met a stellar sales professional who is humble in their approach? That is the core that my parents operate from.

You can imagine the environment this created for me and my siblings. I had a front-row seat to their unfolding business success, and I unknowingly internalized the amazing sales wisdom exuded by my parents. In time, I took a more conscious stance to internalizing their lessons.

Leading up to third grade, everything was great. My grades were all A+, and I soon played the role of Glinda in *The Wizard of Oz*. That was up until September 11, 2001, when everything changed. Living in New York at the time and being raised under the Islamic religion wasn't the easiest.

Not only did the Twin Tower attack mean the whole world was changing around us, as residents of New York, but also the world inside of us. We had to start hiding who we were to strangers and even friends. My mother was forced to take her scarf off to avoid road rage from drivers sharing the same road as us.

As the years progressed and we started to assimilate a bit more with the changing culture, we became US citizens with the help of my mother. From there, my siblings and I all started to grow year after year as individuals, and with that came this need for our parents to become a bit more strict on us. My parents feared we would forget or fail to abide by our cultural and religious rules. They believed they already knew what was best for us; they knew the best plan for our futures, before asking us what we wanted in life. Sound familiar? Of course it does! Every parent in their right mind wants the best for their kids. Every parent wants to take the life lessons they've learned and pass that wisdom down to their kids. They want their kids to be successful, happy, healthy—the whole nine. They only want the best for us, nothing short of it.

Over time, my siblings and I learned to define success, happiness, and health on our own terms. Both brothers proved the idea of having to go to school to be a success was a complete myth. Whereas, my sister and I validated it. Interesting, huh? Of course this raised many questions in our family. What really is success?

From having separate thoughts on success to opinions on lifestyle, race, and religion, my views started to slowly branch off from those of my parents. I'd find myself questioning and comparing American culture to the culture my parents raised me with. I liked some things about American culture and others about Middle Eastern culture. However, I couldn't find myself to be either; I found myself embracing both. One confrontation followed another. In hindsight, though, I saw these were actually blessings in disguise.

The age of eighteen marked a huge stage in my life. It was a year of real-life struggles and difficulties. But it was also a year of tremendous inner growth. I was given the opportunity to put my big girl pants on and really determine the outcome of my life. I went from one school to another, I was alienated from my family, and I was forced to support myself. I soon found the world and the beautiful people in it became the family I always dreamed they would be. During this time, I was thrown into sales as a means of survival. From selling water bottles on Times Square to phone services at T-Mobile, I soon realized I was starting a whole new stage in my life—one that required me to build the rest of my future as a sales professional.

It wasn't long before I realized I was changing. I was becoming more than so-and-so's daughter or the Middle Eastern eighteen-year-old New Yorker. I pushed past every stereotype someone could use to judge me or box me in. I was just like any other human being trying to find her purest self, her destiny, her life, her happiness, her health, and her version of success. Sales helped me go from being the average girl with her fair share of insecurities and self-doubt to a badass young woman who wasn't afraid of a single sour client or objection.

I soon discovered I was living with a fatal tumor in my system, and I broke down one Tuesday afternoon at a friend's home library. I was offered what I like to call "the best medicine," and it not only saved my life but also helped me find myself—the person I'd been looking for all this time. He handed me *The Book of Secrets* by Deepak Chopra, which soon became my holy book, the one and only text I lived by. It introduced me to this beautiful world called Self-Development and opened my eyes to our great world of abundance. I started to realize that my life up to that point had unfolded for a reason, and a good reason at that.

After being accepted to and having to turn down an offer to NYU (my dream school), I soon graduated from community college. I continued my education at the one and only Drexel University, in Center City, Philadelphia. I accepted a dean scholarship there and soon found myself living with foreign exchange students as my roommates. I worked two jobs and attended full-time school to study cultural anthropology. I chose this major, not only because anthropology happened to be the study of humankind—which has always intrigued me—but also because one of my good friends was a biological anthropologist. She later passed away from multiple sclerosis, but during our time together, guess which book I gifted her to help her cope with her condition? I went on from Philadelphia to make my way to the West Coast, where I worked for several start-ups I believed in.
By the age of twenty-two, I had worked a sales career in almost every industry you could think of. The more I sold, the more I became addicted to selling. Just like any other sales role, there were times the pipeline was a bit dry or not ideal. However, I chose to stick with it. I even built my own company, Conscious Lens, as a side project (with just $50 in my bank account). Who said you

can't work and go to school full-time and operate a consulting business?

Conscious Lens was my way of taking the process of self-development and turning it into my lifestyle. From curing myself of the biggest of the big, working through my own insecurities, and living the liberating life I'd always imagined, I decided to share my blessings with the world. Conscious Lens allowed me to create and sell my own self-development consulting services and products. I soon found myself managing employees to take our net from a business that started at $50 to raking in over a six-figure sale. If you'd asked me back then how I did it, I'd probably have a good laugh and respond with the word *purpose*. You see, I had a vision, and no matter how many obstacles *tried* to get in my way, my only option was to succeed in sales.

Sales not only paid my bills—it put me through school and kept my business going. Sales helped me become a better person. Despite how good the money was, I soon realized that I had fallen in love with sales because it *helped solve problems for the modern-day human being*. And this was the moment I realized that we're all salespeople in some capacity. We're all selling something.

It wasn't long before I began applying this realization to every other area of my life. I realized that my inner power and strength was where my confidence came from. I didn't just take my sales cap off whenever I left my employer's office or once I got off a conference call with a client. I kept that sales cap on in class. I applied sales to my personal relationships. I used the principles of sales to get the help of a store clerk as I shopped.

I soon found I could literally have anything and everything I wanted as long as I remained humble, morally stable, curious, and confident in my approach. From there, the world was mine. I'd find a problem and immediately search for a creative solution. Mixing my street smarts and book smarts really went a long way. The rest, as they say, is history.

Reading this book, you will soon realize that I'm not here to just spout the standard or old-school methods of selling. Instead, I'll give you a sneak peek into the mind of someone who learned to master herself through the art of finding herself—and to sell handsomely as a result. Everything I have, I pour into this single purpose: to bring substantial value to the world I so deeply long to serve.

What will you do today to become more purpose-driven?

CHAPTER 1: CONSCIOUS YOU

Great entrepreneurs are risk takers and salespeople at heart. -Barbara Corcoran

What does it take to become an exceptional salesperson? Let's face it: we all have to start somewhere. We don't just start out at the top of our game. It takes work! Going from an average sales professional to an exceptional one within your first six to eight months in the workforce takes a bit more than just being fully aware of your industry, clientele, product, and/or service. It requires the mastery and understanding only provided by self-development.

What's self-development? For those of you who don't know—or know it by its other name, self-improvement—it's simply the study of improving oneself.

You may ask: *So are you trying to tell me I can get better at anything I choose? Well, yes. But before you decide to become a professional in your chosen industry, you must become a better person. Yes, a better human being!*

How do we become better people? Do we have to give to charity or go volunteer? That too, but what I'm referring to here is actually digging deep within, finding the good qualities inside yourself, and getting rid of those attributes and habits that aren't necessary or helpful.

Oh, so you mean I may have to face some things that make me feel uncomfortable? Exactly! Exciting, right?
* Awkward silence. * You see, the key to becoming a better person is being brutally honest with yourself. Not everyone can handle that. But those who want success badly enough and who are willing to stop making excuses are the rare ones who can really make the positive shift in their career. Like a great man once told me, making excuses won't get you paid!

I shared with you in the introduction how my path took me through school, building a sales career, and managing a debilitating health condition. You also know by now that the struggles of that path led me straight to self-development.

My first introduction to the concept was through *The Book of Secrets*. It was the number one tool I used to help get me through some of my toughest times.

The truths I encountered in that book ushered in a new stage in my life. They brought me self-confidence, strength, courage, and resilience. I soon became addicted to working on myself and breaking through the inner blocks I had created some consciously, others subconsciously. I spent every free minute at the local library or Barnes & Noble, sitting on the floor of the self-development section for hours on end. Self-development soon became as important to me as air, water, and food.

I started to realize how much happier I was feeling. I was no longer that girl walking around with her head down, avoiding confrontation. Instead, I was the girl on campus holding her head high, smiling at every passing stranger, hoping to shed some positive light their way.

With the help of self-development and my willingness and desire to better myself, I was able to flip my life around in just under six months. I felt more alive and healthier than ever, despite what was going on around me. When I ran into people from my past, they were constantly asking me:

Gosh, why are you always smiling? What are you so happy about? OMG, are you in love? Yes, you must be in love! Did you get an A on your last test? Why are you so happy? Wait, why? I don't understand! How could you be so happy?

You see, I *was* in love. But not with someone else—with *myself.* Through self-development, I was able to uncover all of my past insecurities, fears, and ignorance. I found my true self and she was someone I could love and admire. I used to feel I wasn't enough. No matter what I did—going to school, getting a degree, becoming a stay-at-home mom—whatever path I was to take, I was bound to fail. Through self-development, I saw that for the lie it was and dropped those thoughts and limiting beliefs to the curb. I found the root of those lies, detached the power they'd once held over me, and liberated myself by pulling that root from under the ground. This not only helped me clean out the unnecessary and negative thoughts I once told myself, chose to believe, and allowed to live inside me, but it also helped me create more room for better, more positive thoughts, emotions, and actions. This *changed* my life.

Once I started to consistently apply every teaching I could get my hands on, I soon became the person I'd always wished to be. I started to truly feel stronger, happier, healthier, more confident, more conscious, more positive—the whole nine! This went on for a few years, right around the same time my sales career started to skyrocket. Now was I satisfied?! I say not! As one of my favorite idols, Bruce Lee, once said, "Be happy, but never satisfied."[1]
With that notion, I started wanting more out of life. I started closing more sales because I could honestly admit that I was getting to know myself better, more deeply than ever before! The closer I got and the more I liked myself, the more I attracted others, resulting in more business in the pipeline.

So what did I do with the world I just opened up inside myself?! I created my baby, Conscious Lens. This was my first legit start-up that drew in more success than I'd imagined. I say this because after attempting a mobile makeup business in both New York City and Philly and an art business while attending school and managing multiple full-time jobs on the side, I understood I would always be a natural entrepreneur. I took it upon myself to create the financial opportunities I dreamed of. I tried it all—anything I found the slightest bit of interest in. Why not? I figured I would have no way of knowing what I'd like until I gave it a try.

Conscious Lens scaled within its first year. I must say I was impressed, and I was spiritually fulfilled. Not only did I build the business with the remaining $50 in my bank account, but I also went from running it myself to hiring six employees, who were all older than me. Two of the people I hired were within my circle of business and did the same consultation work but had no way of scaling or making it a full-time job. By bringing on these two coaches, a marketing assistant, an accountant, an event planner, and another one-on-one consultation scheduling assistant, I made it all happen. We not only offered one- on-one consultations for people all over the world who wanted guidance and/or a support system with their self-development journeys, but we also provided group and event workshops. Most of our services were held online, though a few were held locally and in multiple cities across the US. Although this easily became my full-time job, I found I was never satisfied. I operated CL full time, attended school, grew my sales career, and maintained great health and fitness. Most importantly, I maintained my mental health and kept working on my self-development. The more I worked at it, the more areas I found for improvement.

However, after a few years of dealing with the same issues my clients had, I found myself getting burned out. I no longer found joy in my work or in the business I'd dreamed of owning and operating all my life. Even after taking two vacations and time off, I just couldn't fall back in love with my dream come true.

A few years into feeling this way, I finally decided it was time for an exit strategy. Was I stressed? Ha! ... very. But I realized I needed more. More excitement and challenge, for starters. No matter how hard I tried, I couldn't articulate what was happening. I just kept finding myself having that conversation we've all had with the ex-partner, right? Please know, it's not you (weeping, sniff sniff) ... it's me.

Seriously, though, that's exactly the position I was in. I didn't want anything to do with what I had once built with my own hands, but at the same time, I couldn't fathom not being the young successful business owner and entrepreneur I always envisioned myself to be. I was simply making an unconscious choice. This was a time I was listening to my ego in the wrong way.

Here's the thing about the ego: it's not good or bad. Just like money or anything else in this world, it's not the money or ego that's bad. It's the way we use it. We have a choice—we can either use it properly, or we can misuse it. It's very simple;

subconsciously, I was talking myself out of selling my business, sucking it up to hold onto my once perceived identity.

It wasn't long after this that I realized I was simply denying my own truth and needed to be brutally honest with myself. I only had one life; I had to accept that I was growing as a being and I wanted more. I was entering a new stage. If I wanted more opportunities and growth, I had to embrace the change.

With that self-discovery and realization, I used the power of my strength and my friend, who goes by the name Law of Attraction (LOA), to make it happen. If you've already met LOA, you know it's the immense power within all of us to manifest or attract energies, events, people, and opportunities toward us.

I sat down with myself and literally wrote out exactly how I wanted to close out this chapter in my life in the most positive and beneficial manner possible. I wanted to find a business that could continue employing all my workers and take care of all the clients we had acquired over the years. It was a very sensitive subject for me to even think about. It was hard to trust many folks at this time. I tried anything and everything I could to make sure this was done in the most ethical way possible.

After conducting countless interviews and reviewing numerous business proposals, with the grace of my creative powers (more on this later), I manifested the perfect candidate. One of my own coaches, who I'd sought guidance from, happened to be the one. I was truly blessed. After a few meetings, we closed the deal. I not only manifested the perfect fit for my clients, former employees, and my former business, but I was also able to take home over six figures. But that just marked the beginning for me. I continued to build my sales career, using everything I'd learned from my experience with Conscious Lens in my sales roles. I went back to being a full-time employee, figuring it would be a good way for me to get more sales skills and expertise under my belt while allowing me time to whip up my next creation.

Months later, I finally decided to make a trip out to New York to visit my family. It was time, especially after I'd been away for so long. One idea after another popped into my head, and I just couldn't get my mind off serving humanity in a positive way. I realized money was everywhere; the avenues of income one could generate were endless. However, I wanted to rake in the dough by impacting the human race in the most positive way possible. I was deciding on what to do next while keeping my priority to serve humanity top of mind.

After making my way back to the West Coast, I came across a hackathon flyer on campus. If you don't know, a hackathon is a competition that takes place over the course of twenty-four to forty-eight hours, where coders get together and try to come up with new and innovative ideas for tech products. And the lucky winners take home a prize. So I figured, *Hey, why not? I love people. People love me. Let's get out there!* As this was my first hackathon, I didn't know it was a forty-eight-hour competition. My teammates kept giving me funny looks, and somebody finally addressed the elephant in the room:

"Hey, where's your camping bag?"

"What camping bag?"

"We have to stay overnight for this? It's a 48hr hackathon, you know?"

"Wait, what? Look, dude, I'm a psych major! I'm just here to network. Plus,

I have plans tonight!"

Now, despite not being able to stay the night or not being a computer science major, I saw the advantage. I simply saw the opportunity and used it to help our team. My upper hand was that I was able to bring my psych, business, and sales skills to offer something unique to the table. With a team of five coders and myself, we were able to create an app for kids struggling with ADHD. Hours into the work and staring at empty water bottles and bags of chips, we created the one and only winner.

Though our pitch was cut short, we were still able to win the competition. Phew, what a relief! From the huge success we shortly received from investors and potential team members and managers, we grew our venture. But just like any other team, we needed members who had the time to invest in it. However, that didn't work out with our group, so we had no choice but to sell our design and go our separate ways. It was yet another stage in our lives that we naturally outgrew. What we took away from the collaboration was more than just the finances; it was also the advanced expertise and experience.

Years later, I tried my hand at many other projects and eventually found myself writing this book while working on an online platform, which I will be sure to share with you in the near future.

What will you do differently today to build that loyal relationship you've always envisioned having with yourself?

1 "Bruce Lee Quotable Quotes," Goodreads, accessed January 17, 2019, https://www.goodreads.com/quotes/19527-be-happy-but-never-satisfied.

CHAPTER 2: **THE REAL MONEY**

Become addicted to constant and never-ending self-improvement. -Anthony J. D'Angelo

Self-development

We started this book talking about self-development for one simple reason: At the heart of sales is the reality that you aren't just selling a product—you're selling yourself. All along my entrepreneurial journey, sales has continuously shown up in both my life and career. No matter what industry I focus my skills on, or what product and/or service I'm selling, the underlying truth is the same: I'm always selling myself. My character, my personality, my style of selling, my accent (that NY accent does creep up on me from time to time), my syntax, the way I carry myself—the whole package. Just like when I turn the tables and play the customer role, I expect to deal with a professional who has a sense of confidence about them that's unmatched by their competitors. When they meet this expectation, I'm more willing to hear them out and open myself to the possibilities, ideas and value they could bring to the table.

Having that expectation for sales professionals who approach me, I give off the same presence in return. As the Golden Rule states, "Treat others the way you want to be treated." Not only is it a rule of life, but it's also a major rule in sales.

When you read the words *confident, strong, professional, charismatic, courageous, trustworthy, respectful, helpful, admirable, prompt, loyal,* what or who comes to mind? On a scale of 1–10, how would you rate yourself in regard to these attributes? Ten being you strongly exhibit this attribute, whereas one means you struggle to exhibit this attribute. I'm assuming you're reading this book to become better in sales and in life, right? Okay, then do yourself a favor and be honest with your answers. The more honest you are with yourself, the further you will go in life. Go ahead and track your score below:

- Confident
- Strong
- Professional
- Charismatic
- Courageous
- Trustworthy
- Respectful
- Helpful
- Admirable
- Prompt
- Loyal

How did you score? On any of these you marked a 5 or lower, get working on it. On any of these you marked a 5 or higher, get working on it. No matter where you scored, know that there will ALWAYS be room for growth. Even if you're number one in what you do, you still have work to do. Yes, you're ahead of most of your competition, but you want to maintain that level of excellence, and at any point, the number one spot can be taken.

You're probably wondering: *Why are we even talking about this? Why are we talking about becoming a better person and becoming confident and loyal and helpful, etc.?* It's simple—we want more sales *and* long-lasting, quality sales to come in. To achieve this, we have to carry ourselves with integrity and see value in who we are as a human being before we expect strangers to see the same in us, let alone trust us enough to hand over their credit cards. The attributes listed above are the same we should be evaluating in every relationship—both personal and professional. Think of the foundational relationships in your life, those that have given you tremendous growth. Chances are high that they too acquired these same attributes.

The same applies to the most important relationship you'll ever have. I'm talking about your relationship with yourself. No matter what you tell yourself, good or bad, most likely it's written all over your face and is obvious for all to see. The energy we put off about others says a lot about what we think of ourselves. And what we see in others tends to be a reflection of what we see in ourselves. For example, you see a not-so-attractive trait in another person, chances are you have or feel that you have the same inside yourself. On the other hand, if you see the good in someone and can't help but be inspired by their courage—well, you can easily see the same in yourself. It's very simple; it's almost as if we humans walk around with an invisible two-sided mirror glued to our faces, yet we don't know it.

The more we start to accept a growth and abundance mindset, the more we will find ourselves focusing on the possibilities of feeling better about ourselves. Soon those rare great days become the norm.   You see, self-development is about uncovering all the possibilities, talents, and gold that's been living inside of you this entire time. It's about finding your inner strengths and bringing them back to life!
But why should I have to "develop" myself?
Are you trying to say there is something wrong with me?
Wait, you're not talking about me, right? You're talking about your other readers, aren't you?

Here's the thing: There is nothing wrong with self-development and/or those who choose to practice it. In fact, everything about it is great! If you were to study any successful professional, in any field, you'll notice they're a firm believer in self-development. Simply put, choosing to become a better or the best [fill in the title here], requires that a person decide to become the best version of themselves.

None of us were put here to be slaves to our negative thoughts and limiting beliefs. We weren't born to suffer emotionally, mentally, physically, even financially. Don't worry—in later chapters, I'll share my secrets of financial success with you; but the self-development work has to come first. It's the foundation from which our wealth is built. We were put here to be the best Stacy, the best Bauer, the best John, the best Nancy—fill in the blank—we can be. But let's take a minute to address the Negative Nancy's.

- *I don't know why I have to work on myself when there's nothing to work on.*
- *I'm perfectly okay with going to my nine-to-five, doing the bare minimum just to keep my job. I mean, I love rushing home to crash on the couch in front of my awesome flat-screen!*
- *Yay, what she said! We don't need to fix ourselves! There's nothing to fix! We're comfortable with the amount of money we make. But, hey, we'd take more if it was offered!*
- *Better life—what could that possibly mean? I love my crappy job and my wife, who I can't stand, and my friends, who I only like when we drink together.*
- *Yay! Screw this whole "working on myself" thing! I'm better off watching TV and hanging out with friends. I'm okay with my problems right now! They'll figure themselves out eventually.*

- *My finances? No worries about that! If that doesn't work out, I can just cry to Mommy and Daddy (despite being over the age of eighteen) and expect them to pay for my bills and hand over the moola! (I mean they always do, so ...).*

PHEW! You done yet? Let's get serious here. The rest of your life is in front of you. What you find interest in at this stage of your life determines how you move forward. If you settle for an average job, that's as far as you'll go. Whoever you look up to is who you will become. But if you spend most of your life trying to impress people, those insecurities will have to be tamed. Sooner or later that shallowness will catch up to you.

Now, if what I'm saying doesn't register with you, please do yourself a favor—open your mind to the idea of creating a better life for yourself, or hand this book over to a growth-seeker who may appreciate the message. No need for us to continue feeding into the little fables we tell ourselves. Simply put, nobody has time to waste. You don't, and I sure don't. Glad we're on the same page there.

Let's imagine how much more fulfilling, happy, and positive would our lives be if we were to just make a few adjustments here and there? Every time you notice a negative, selfish, or lack-driven thought race through your mind, immediately drop the belief you once tied to it and replace it with one that's more self-fulfilling.

Every time you see someone you know succeed or do well in something that's important to them, instead of disliking them or trying to bring them down, you could actually get inspired by their success and show your support and love.

Every time you see a physically attractive individual that happens to be within your age bracket and gender, instead of showing hatred or bringing them down or trying to ignore them, face them and show them kindness and friendliness instead.

Every time someone treats you with anything negative— whether that be hatred, disrespect, or malice—instead of doing to them what they did to you, walk away with peace. Remember this: You weren't put on this planet to treat anyone as if they're less worthy than you. You were put here to represent the lesson by being the example you want to convey.

You might think I don't live in the twentieth century and that I'm not aware of how nasty and unconscious we human beings can *choose* to act at times. I chuckle. Trust me, coming from some of the most violent and crime-driven neighborhoods in New York City and Philly has certainly shaped me to know a thing or two. I know that environment all too well. The point here is not to reciprocate negative behavior. Rather, be aware of it and stand back with love. As we all know, we can't fight fire with fire and expect to get anywhere with it. Show love. Be love.

Life is too short and precious for us to settle, to be unhappy, unfulfilled, unhealthy—you know the drill. In fact, we *all* know this truth, yet we *choose* to be completely oblivious to it. We all know that our life can end at any moment! It can end before we get through reading this book. It can end before we eat our next meal. It can end before we tell our loved ones we love them. It can end before we give our precious fur-babies the best organic treats in the world. Life just isn't worth living in any way that's not profiting to us *and* to those around us.

I'm all for self-love and the *doing-you policy,* trust me. But you see, there's a huge difference in being selfish—not giving two *apples* about anyone else— and in giving yourself attention, care, love, and positive self-affirmations. There's a meaning behind that.

When we work on ourselves and take care of our needs in a genuine and positive way, we become our natural selves again! By "natural selves," I mean we become the human beings we once were when we were happy-go-lucky kiddos running around in our diapers! We become pure in heart and genuine with our intentions. Whether it be in our personal or professional relationships, we lead by truth—by being and *choosing* to exist with truth.

Self-esteem

You know, we're all really the same. We all want to be happy. We all want to have money and be well-off in one way or another. We all want to live in a beautiful and comfortable home and environment. We all want to one day have a family we can share our success, life, and abundance with. So let's stop telling ourselves we are in a rat race and that if the next person is successful and living the life of their dreams, they're stealing from us. There is simply no need for that foolishness.

The raw reality is that there is more abundance than we realize out there in this amazing universe we live in. The funny part is that this has *always* been the case. Yet, as humans, we feel the need to be envious whenever we come across someone who is smarter, more attractive, or even younger than us.

Now why is that? Why do we feel the need for such pitiful thoughts and feelings? My guess is this one great word called *self-esteem*. Life is very simple, and with that comes the simplicity of awareness. When you start to become more self-aware, and more conscious, you'll recognize and read people better than ever before. Better yet, you'll be able to read your own negative patterns! To me, growing self-esteem is as important in life as maintaining multiple streams of livelihood. I'm talking about self-worth, value, and confidence.

This beautiful door to a life of possibilities is certainly worth the effort. Now, before we dig into the topic, let's not get it confused with cockiness. Understanding your self-worth is not the same thing as being full of yourself. Anyone who believes them to be the same is really just lying to themselves. So don't believe anyone who misunderstands what confidence and self-esteem really mean. Please do yourselves a favor and reconsider taking any sort of advice from someone who lacks self-esteem.

I'm speaking from experience here. Family members, friends, coworkers— anyone in your circle can try to influence you in ways that don't serve you. These are people who hope to control you, sometimes even unconsciously. Some are conscious of their insecurities, but most don't have the slightest idea or interest in admitting this truth to themselves or to anyone around. Here's a simple scenario to illustrate what I mean (names have been changed to preserve privacy):

Meet Connor, a thirty-seven-year-old accountant. His personal and professional relationships are okay—he neither hates nor loves anyone in his life. He loves to ski and golf. He is an avid novel reader and video game player.

Meet Larry, a thirty-two-year-old grad fresh from med school. He loves all of his friends and family and is a true social butterfly. He loves to play soccer and hang out with his cat, Stan (also known as, Stan the Man).

Larry gets his first job out of college as a veterinary technician, and two years in, he starts to regret the career path he chose. He considers other options he might possibly qualify for without having to add too much to his student loans. One day he comes across a job offer to get into the beautiful world of real estate. After being accepted into the brokerage he thinks will be most interesting and beneficial, he meets up with his friend Connor the following night.

The friends update each other on what's going on their lives. Connor didn't have much to share besides the fact that the eggs were on sale over at the local grocery store—bummer none of us knew. When it's Larry's turn, he can't contain his excitement. He explains how much he's looking forward to his new gig and how he can't wait to start the following week. Immediately, Connor decides to give his two cents—without being asked, of course—and starts to convince Larry that he's making a bad decision. He addresses all of his concerns and tries his hardest to make it sound like he has the best intentions for Larry's career. In truth, he's projecting his own fears from a time he thought he wanted to work in the same industry but was turned away by doubts his dad instilled in him.

Without knowing any of this, poor Larry starts to believe Connor's limiting beliefs. He starts to reconsider the real estate opportunity. He leaves dinner feeling dejected, quite the opposite of the excitement he felt when he arrived at the restaurant.

However, a day or two passes and he starts to feel that same level of excitement he felt when he first considered real estate. Despite the mixed feelings (due to Connor's fears), Larry decides to ignore all of those limiting beliefs and listen to his intuition. Eventually, this leads him into the brokerage that same day. Six months go by, and Larry finds himself being the number one real estate broker in the company he works for. From there, he decides to branch off and start his own brokerage. Two years strong, he hires a solid group of employees and becomes top in his city. Not only does he laugh at himself when he thinks back to that miserable conversation he had with Conner—seven years later, Connor hires him to help sell his previous home and buy one of Larry's. Who knows what would've happened if Larry had only listened to the limiting and fear-driven perception of his friend, Connor.

I'm not saying you have to be wary of every person in your life. You know plenty of nice, safe, and caring people. What I'm saying is, be aware of people who are not conscious enough to work on and detach their fears, insecurities, and limiting beliefs from those around them. Unlike Larry, who was the lucky one— listening to his intuition and pursuing what he knew was the path for him —there are many people out there who choose to listen to and adopt the fears of others. This only results in lost opportunities and forgotten dreams.

The moral of the story is this: don't take advice from those who don't have (or don't *yet* have) the life you want. I'm not talking about taking advice only from a doctor if you want to be a doctor. I'm saying, take ALL advice with a grain of Himalayan salt (trust me, it's better than Morton's). Seriously though, apply the same strategy even to what you're reading in this book! Not every piece of advice will apply to every single person in every situation. But be open to the advice and acknowledge that we are all students of this beautiful game called life.

Think about what you see when you look in the mirror. Do you see a person of strength, hustle, gratitude, peace, intelligence, and logic? Or do you choose to see the opposite when you stare back into that good-looking mirror of yours? Side note, the mirror was never that good-looking. (We made it good-looking). Boom! That's your girl, confidence, speaking!

The way we choose to see ourselves says everything about how others see us. Just like every other part of life, it's very simple and self-explanatory. Pretty cut 'n' dry, huh?

Sure is, but we don't make it that simple, do we? We overcomplicate it by believing the lies we tell ourselves. The funny thing about these fables is how much energy and effort we put into perpetuating them—how hard we work to convince ourselves that these lies are our reality. Then we go about our lives acting as if the crap inside our minds is the truth and nothing but the truth! Lies, lies, and more lies. How about we switch it up for a bit? Let's just run a little experiment here. Let's say for one whole day you only took in and accepted the raw reality of your life. How much different would today be from yesterday? How much more liberating, positive, and lighter would your life be if you applied that strategy to the rest of your life? I get it. It's not the easiest thing to just stop cold turkey. It's not that easy to just stop lying to yourself. Ouch. Were you ready for that last sentence? Doesn't matter. We must stop the crap we feed ourselves, once and for all.

We weren't put here to contemplate life and think *what if this* or *what if that...*

- That last girl who was supposed to go on a date with you who disappeared? *Her loss!*
- That company that promised they'd hire you under the agreed-upon salary but never came through? *Their loss!*
- That employee who promised they wouldn't be late after the third time? Their loss!
- That person (doesn't matter their gender, age, or significance in your life) who didn't see your worth? *Their loss!*

You see the pattern here, right? It's not our loss, rather our gain when we choose to make the simple decision to move forward in life. I get it: sometimes life throws us lessons we may not be ready for. But crying like a four-year-old (even though you call yourself an adult) doesn't fix anything! In fact, it only makes matters worse. Yes, sometimes you need to cry a river. But let me tell you something before you decide to. Think about all of the under-eye wrinkle creams and procedures you'll have to spend your hard-earned money on for such foolishness? That's your call, but I like my wrinkle-free under-eye skin, my cold hard cash, and my badass inner self.

Ain't nobody got time for that nonsense! Unfortunately, we all have time for nonsense, hence why so many people waste their lives focusing on things that won't get them anywhere. But none of my readers fall into that category, do they? You guys can be the judge of that.

The reality is, we are all given a series of choices to make throughout the course of our precious lives. We can choose to sleep in, or we can choose to go chase that sun up. We can choose to believe the BS we tell ourselves, or we can accept the truth and start living a conscious and real life. We can work on those six-pack abs or just lie to ourselves and say it's not worth it. We can train for that marathon and force ourselves to do bigger and better things, or we can just choose to be lazy and grab that greasy, MSG-filled processed meal-on-the-go. We can choose to invest our money in causes we love and triple our funds, or we can choose to spend every dime we have on designer clothing that costs more than our monthly housing. Our lives are simply made up of choices.

And the truth is, those choices determine the path we walk through the rest of our lives. Let me ask you this: when you look in the mirror, what do you see? Or, what do you *choose* to see?

I Am Deserving of Only Good

Once we start to make the right decisions in choosing to see the good in ourselves, we enter the next stage in truth and self-discovery. Everyone who's choosing the right decision in reading this book will soon realize the meaning of what a true and valuable life really means to them. They will start to notice, evaluate, and raise their bar in one area of life to another.

But before you can take it to that level of consciousness, you have to take a step back and make sure you truly believe what you are reading here. Are you capable of and worthy of a better life, a better career, a better relationship, a better purpose? I hope so! Now be honest with yourself. On a scale of one to ten, how worthy and deserving do you feel of gaining a better (fill in the blank—it's your life here, and you make the rules). Now, repeat after me:

• I am deserving of a better life.

- I am deserving of financial freedom and prosperity.
- I am deserving of a great relationship with myself, my spouse, my family, my friends, etc.
- I am deserving of a positive mindset.
- I am deserving of a great life that makes me happy.
- I am deserving of a life that's fulfilling.
- I am deserving of a life that's meant to inspire others.
- I am deserving of a life that works in my favor, to be of positive service to others.
- I am deserving of love.
- I am deserving of happiness.
- I am deserving of success.
- I am deserving of inner and outer peace.
- I am deserving of living a truth-filled life.
- I am deserving of freedom in all areas of my life.
- I am deserving of [whatever else satisfies your precious being].

Feeling better? Glad to hear it! When you start to feel good about yourself inside and out, you will naturally share your good energy with others as well. You will open new chapters in your life and really make a difference, not only in your life but also in the lives of those around you. You'll notice how much you are smiling and how much good you're putting into the world. You will give of yourselves wholeheartedly to both the projects and individuals you decide to invest your time in.

All those past limiting beliefs and emotions will start to fade away, slowly but surely. Before you know it, more and more positives will start to flow your way. Whether its positive individuals, opportunities, experiences, and or goals you start to accomplish, it will all be sent your way. Not only that, but it will work in your favor with ease. It will no longer be difficult for you to be positive, *genuinely* happy, successful, and generous with your knowledge and resources. You will be so delighted and happy with your life that you'll want to share it with others in hopes of inspiring them to live a fulfilled and happy life too.

Imagine that. Imagine a life where you can be all of those things and much more. Imagine living the life you've always dreamed of. Imagine having everything you've always wanted. Imagine being the person you've always wanted to be. Imagine a life of true abundance in all areas. Well, guess what? That person can be you, and that life can be yours to keep.

How could that be possible, Bauer? I have so many problems in my life, blah blah blah.

As the great Bruce Lee once said: *Empty your mind. Be formless, shapeless—like water. Now you put water into a cup, it becomes the cup. You put water into a bottle, it becomes the bottle. You put it in a teapot, it becomes the teapot. Now water can flow, or it can crash. Be water, my friend.*[2]

Don't be confused by Lee's teaching here; it's very simple. What he's really saying is to be like water: adaptable to the situations and experiences you're put into. Now, if you understand the power of individual intention, you'll soon know that we all create our own situations, experiences, opportunities and even "problems." (I put quotation marks around the word *problems* because that's just what we perceive them to be, for good or bad reasons of our own choosing.) Be like water; go with the flow on living a better life and making the conscious decision to be the best version of yourself that you can possibly be.

Let's face it, we've all had issues in our lives—past hurts and tribulations that we forced ourselves to get over. Some of us are still working through these struggles. Of course, we don't want to bathe in our own self-pity and sorrow. Rather, we want to acknowledge these issues in our lives, recall them only when necessary, and give them power only when there is a positive reason to do so. From there, we show our gratitude for the multiple lessons we've derived from them, and we can use them to strengthen us. Use them to invoke positivity and abundance into our lives. You've probably heard it before, *take a negative and turn it into a positive.*

We can all agree this is easier said than done. But the key here isn't to focus on what is out of our control; focus on those areas where you do have control and choose to take strategic action. Focus all your energy and thoughts on what good you can make of these frustrating issues, obstacles, and pains you've *allowed* and made the unconscious *decision* to throw away the limited time you have toward them.

You've heard the saying, "Life is too short." If you believe it, why not abide by it at all times? Is it because you *just don't feel like it*? You don't care about the truth and don't want to hear about it? Or is it because you get comfortable with the old thought patterns and continue feeding them into your subconscious mind —because it's easier? Only you can answer that question and make daily decisions accordingly. This determines the results you'll see, feel, and experience.

You can either choose to live with mediocrity, accept being overweight, stay in debt—list any other socially acceptable issue here—like most of the Western world, or you can make the conscious decision to create a better life. A life where you choose to change what was once comfortable to you, where you decide to live a life of abundance, where you grow from what once held you back, where you take action and decide what life you want to live and become happier, healthier, more successful. I'm talking about becoming abundant and prosperous in every way.

If there's anything I'd like for you to take away from this section of the book, it would be this: We all have a very significant power within us— the power of *decision*. The type of decisions you make day in and day out all count at the end of the day. Whether or not they work in your favor, is up to you.

Law of (Beautiful) Attraction

Do you remember when you were a kid and you really wanted a certain toy, but your parents wouldn't buy it for you? But with the strategic and unconscious genius sales power that all kids have, you were able to get it in your possession? Haha! Yes, we've all been there. Even for those of us who didn't come from the most privileged family, we've all experienced this in one form or another.

Maybe you've heard of the Law of Attraction, you believe in it, or you live by it entirely. Or you might have heard of it and understand it, but you don't really apply it to your life. Wherever you fall on the spectrum, you can recognize it whenever it's brought up as the subject of conversation.

For starters, let's discuss and further dissect what the Law of Attraction really means. My team and I conducted a poll, asking readers how they would define the Law of Attraction. Here are a few responses we gathered:

LOA is when:
- *we get things we hope and pray for*
- *we write down something we want to happen*

- *we speak into existence and passionately ask for something we desire we ask and expect to receive in return what we focus on*
- *we expect what we ask for and nothing less*

The reality and truth behind the Law of Attraction is a combination of all these. Still, it needs a bit more explanation. The *Law of Attraction* (LOA) is simply a belief that needs to be acted upon in order to be validated or come to fruition. For example, let's say I play tennis (which, I do from time to time) and I have a match coming up within the next month. My goal here would be to beat my opponent. In this case, I can either just focus on the goal or I can repeat out loud on a daily basis, *I will win my tennis match. I will win my tennis match.*

Would that be LOA? Yes, but not entirely. You see, LOA is more than just focusing on, writing down, and/or praying with intention to achieve a goal. LOA is about pairing that power of belief and faith with the power of action. When we act upon our goals and dreams and couple that with faith in our own abilities— that's when we start to really use LOA in full effect.

You may be familiar with the movie *The Secret*, which explains LOA in more detail. If you haven't seen the movie or read the book, I highly encourage you to do so. It will help you understand this way of thinking even more.

Now, why am I talking about LOA? Here's the thing...
When it comes to getting anything you want in life, achieving it boils down to a few simple and fundamental elements:

1. Come to realize and admit to yourself that you want something.Whether it's an experience or even a person to be your significant other and/or friend, you have to start by naming the thing you want.

2. Announce it. Tell others about your desire. Write it down and read it every day. Or just think about it day in and day out.

3. Put in the action. Whatever it takes is what you will do to achieve the results you're looking for. This step includes completing the short-term goals in order to achieve the long-term success. Whether it's practicing for a game, looking up cooking recipes online, writing your thesis, etc., you have to put in the work.

4. Couple the action steps that you're actively working on with an undeniable amount of faith and belief that you will achieve your goal.

5. Continue to apply faith and action for as long as it takes to achieve your goal.

6. To make the process easier on yourself (especially if it's a massive goal you're wanting to accomplish), reach out to people you respect to support you throughout your journey.

Building a close tribe with other positive beings who are actively pursuing their goals and dreams is the best way to go. There is no better feeling than to have a group of solid human beings on top of their game to connect with. As they say, we become who we spend the most time with, so choose wisely.

7. Boom! Achieve that goal. Then set your bar higher next time around. Share your success with others, and inspire them to repeat it over and over again. That's it! Just rinse and repeat. Rinse and repeat.

The more you practice it, the easier and more natural it becomes. Of course, you can apply this to any area of your life. Just be sure to pair your intention with *unwavering faith* (as the one and only Lisa Nichols put it). Proper action and preparation are needed to bring your goals into being. It's as simple as that.

Bob Proctor said it best in his book *The Art of Living*, The ruling mental state is everything. Our inner faculties are where it's really happening. Not outside of us. What you think produces your life. This is the art of living.

LOA has become mainstream. More and more people are acknowledging and applying it, and it's making headway in Hollywood. Celebrities, icons, and athletes are joining in. Will Smith, Jim Carrey, Kanye West, Lisa Nichols, Bob

Proctor, Conor McGregor, and Big Sean—just to name a few—have begun to champion LOA. These folks have not only praised the message through their music and in interviews but also in multiple movies, shows, books, and seminars.

It's gone from being a novel idea to a belief that is transforming the way people live. Millions of people are practicing LOA every single day, and little do they know how powerful and prominent its effect is on their lives.

The cool part about LOA isn't just the knowledge that we all create and manifest what we focus on, put action into, and believe in, but that it's also a tool to help you attract more abundance and good into your life. The more you focus on goals that encourage you to better yourself, the more you grow. Remember earlier in the book when we were speaking about deserving good in our lives and focusing on becoming a better, healthier, and happier version of ourselves? Well, with the power of LOA, we can make it happen now more than ever, being that we're not only aware of the fact that we can grow into our best selves but that we understand how to accomplish it.

On the other hand, LOA can move a person in a negative direction. Due to its effectiveness and power, a person with a lack mindset can attract distressing issues into their lives. For example: Let's take a peek at Miss Negative Nancy and the thoughts that roam her mind regarding her daily life.

Last we heard about her, she was stressing about her overdue bills, her children who she can't control, her job that she hates, the fact that she's single and there are *no good men left,* and her weight that she can't seem to manage. Her life motto is: *Same sh**, different day.* You know the drill.

Now if you were given the opportunity to interact with Miss Negative Nancy, what do you expect you'd hear from her? More about the recent bill she received in the mail and her kids flunking out of high school. The list goes on and on and on. You avoid her so you don't have to hear about all the mess she continues to entertain herself with.

Do you notice the pattern here? The more she focuses on these temporary issues, the more she will continue to manifest them, time and time again. Soon enough, these temporary problems she's having will turn into permanent problems, being that seems to be all she's focused on. No surprise there.

On the other hand, we have Miss Positive Penny. Like Miss Negative Nancy, she is thirty-eight years old. Now, Penny is a true believer in good energy, happiness, and health. She lives by the motto: *Give good, get good.* Penny is just like any other ordinary lady—she has her set of obstacles in her marriage, career, social life, health, and so on. However, she chooses not to focus too much on her issues. Instead, she stays focused on her faith and contributes her efforts to making them better. Not a day goes by that she's not smiling from cheek to cheek. Whenever you run into Penny, she's as cheerful and kind as can be. Penny continues to live with a happy and cheerful attitude about her day-to- day experiences and chooses to turn her pet peeves into strengths.

Just like Negative Nancy and Positive Penny, we've all had days that didn't go exactly the way we wanted, but it's not about comparing our obstacles to those of everyone around us. It's about understanding that we *all* have the same power to choose our battles wisely. You can look at them as obstacles or just pop quizzes that life throws at you from time to time—like in school when you decided to hate that one teacher because she surprised you with a pop quiz the moment the bell rang to start class. Life is the same way: filled with pop quizzes, and it sure doesn't matter whether or not we like them. So we'd better get used to those pop quizzes and realize they are *only* here to help us grow and become a better version of ourselves. In other words, this is the time when everything we've learned from all those self-development books comes in handy.

Show Me the Money

Now that we have a firm understanding of what self-development and Law of Attraction truly mean, we can be sure to apply them to our livelihoods. Being that readers come to this book with experience in multiple different industries, let's talk about how we can all add more digits to that bank account with what we've learned so far.

Before we move forward, though, let's define what *money* really means to you. What kind of emotions, thoughts, and actions can you recall when you think of the word *money*? Does it force you to feel guilty, bad, or even selfish for thinking about it? Or do you feel deserving, abundant, positive, and confident when you think about the money you have? How you answer the question determines how much money you have and if you're in the danger zone or the prosperous zone.

You see, the way you choose to think of money has a lot to do with your past, your upbringing, family members, friends, teachers, and other authority figures. Just like anything else, you have to really sit down and discover if your perceptions are fostering or hindering your growth and the goals you want to achieve. So if you choose to listen to the story about how rich people are mean and selfish and how it's a bad thing to have a plethora of money, then you've got some work to do.

Money is a continual form of energy that exists within every human life. It helps us secure a place to live, feed our bodies nutritious meals, take care of our loved ones, prepare for a rainy day, and support the needs of our community.

You've heard "Mo Money Mo Problems." In that case, money takes on a negative connotation. We've seen and heard it all. We've seen people act different or suddenly superior because of their newfound fame and glamour. We've seen relationships burned due to the lack of loyalty; wars have even broken out over financial issues.

So is money bad or good? Mo Money Mo Solutions? Neither! Just like any other thing in this beautiful world, it's not the money that's good or bad. It's the way people choose to use it. We can either use money for all the great things it can provide our lives, or we can abuse it and throw it all away the second it comes into our possession. Again, it's not the money we should focus on, it's the responsibility and decisions of the user. We are held accountable for our beliefs about money. It's not our job to bring others down for the unconscious decisions they make. Rather, our job is to become better versions of ourselves so we can naturally inspire others to do the same.

Should we work to earn money and continue wanting more? Absolutely! Money is a great tool to have! It doesn't necessarily define happiness, but it sure is one of the keys to happiness! With money, we can fulfill all of our basic needs, the needs of those we care about, build multiple streams of passive income, and more! We can achieve all the goals and dreams we've been putting on hold due to lack of time and money. But is this true? Or is this just an excuse we tell ourselves? We can build that dream business we've always wanted or that dream lifestyle we've always wished for.

Money is a great thing to have, and having tons of it is even better! Speaking of the middle-class mindset, Grant Cardone, says it best... He explains this class system as the "mental trap." You know, the need to feel like you should live like every other average Joe: Go to school, get a degree, work for someone you dislike, buy a house and a car, get married and have a few kids while you're at it. Keep adding more and more debt to your name, and try to keep up with the lazy Jones's.

What I take away from his teaching is this: by having money work for you, you learn to treat your money as one of many sources coming your way. Instead of relying on one source of income and choosing to believe that it's "safe," accept that it's actually what's most risky. Let's just make sure we're keeping our morals and character in alignment with the money we're striving for.

Whatever your motives may be with money, keep it moral here. What does "having money" mean to you? The goal is to take this financial abundance and use it for a good cause. I mean if I were to give you a million dollars right now, what would you do with it? Go with your first instinct on each and circle below:

1. Pay off rent/mortgage for the next 24 months.

2.Buy a Lamborghini and show it off to the hotties you

want to impress.

3. Buy a franchise.

4. Increase your spending for the next five years (maybe) because you can.

5. Create an innovative tool to give back to a cause that's important to you.

6. Other.

If you're a pretty conscious being, you'll notice what I just did there. I alternated between a conscious decision and an unconscious one. The idea wasn't necessarily to confuse you but to challenge you to admit who you truly are. You see, what we decide to do with money once it comes into our possession determines not only our self-worth (internally), but how financially free and/or stable we are.

Are we just shallow people who only care about how others see us, or do we have a deeper calling inside of us? Do we buy nice things to show people our status, or is it just a nice article of clothing we choose to wear for our own benefit? Whatever the motive, the goal isn't to get too caught up in it; rather, we should just enjoy the luxuries our money can buy.

Now don't get me wrong, I love nice things. Nice cars, homes, shades, jewelry, clothing—you name it. Still, they do not define me to me. I say *"define me to me"* because the opinion of others doesn't really matter. I know what my value is—not only to myself but to everyone I come in contact with. I know what I bring to the table. With that, I know that what I wear or what car I choose to drive doesn't make me any better or worse of a person. It just so happens to be a nice form of transportation to get me from point A to B; that's all it is. Now, yes, I may decide to name my baby (Naz). Don't you name your car? But again, it doesn't mean anything more than just that to me. I, Bauer, determine who I am —both to myself and to the world. Period.

Consider this for a second: What if a person has all the nice things in the world but still treats people with the utmost respect? This person is happy, successful, and has every material thing they've always wanted. Do you think there would still be a good number of folks who would take these blessings for granted? Of course! You see, it's not about what we have or don't have that determines how happy, successful, or fulfilled we are. It's about what lives inside of us that determines what lives outside and around us. When we have an undeniable faith in our abilities, everything changes. We start to not only attract opportunities (material and non-material), we also start to actually *become* the person we've always dreamed of being. We have everything we need inside of us, and we feel like we're on top of the world. Not that we're better than anyone else but just on top of our world. We feel great about ourselves, continue to stay on top of our internal work, and have all the external possessions we find value in.

Remember, there's nothing wrong with owning nice, luxurious items. They can help us save time, make our daily lives more efficient, and even relieve some unnecessary stress from our shoulders. So again, it's how and why we use them, and important that we don't abuse them. We are all ever-evolving students in life, and feedback is sometimes the best blessing others can share with us. Just like when we feel deserving of self-esteem and great self-worth, we can be deserving of nice things and money as well. Once we tell ourselves that we have earned the right to take possession of such items, we can say that we can have anything and everything our heart desires.

Thinking about the goals at the forefront of your mind may bring up the question: *Who am I?* Before you start to act on your career goals, you may find yourself questioning your worth in society, wondering what you are capable of accomplishing. Can you become a top physician in the hospital? Can you become the top entrepreneur in your local area? Can you become the top sales rep at the company or companies you represent? *Heck yes, you can!*

The funny thing about LOA is how quickly it can begin to work for you once you've gotten a firm understanding and application of it in your life. As soon as you start to really *believe* it and integrate it into your lifestyle, you will start to manifest it all, and I mean *all*. Let me share a few stories with you here. Instead of sharing every single manifestation story with you, I'll just briefly cover some of the most prominent ones from my life.

1. Vision: Since I was a little girl, my family and I would visit Times Square on occasion. I would point up at the NYU signs and tell my parents I was going to get accepted to NYU one day. **Result:** Despite all obstacles, I made it into my dream school. And there ain't no telling how I made it happen besides utilizing the unwavering belief I always had in myself.

2. Vision: Watching business women walk back and forth on Wall Street, I told myself that I would one day be the sole owner or co-owner of a profitable business. **Result:** I became a business owner of a very profitable business at the age of nineteen and again at twenty-three. And who knows how many more times I'll make that happen?!

3. Vision: I was diagnosed with a condition that affected every area of my mind, body, and soul, but I was determined not to let it take my life away and control my waking years. **Result:** I fought the condition away, by feeding my mind with nutritious thoughts and abundant beliefs and by practicing both self- development and LOA on a daily basis.

4. Vision: I've always wanted to model and showcase mynon-verbal sales abilities by using my God-given features. I hoped it would be another form of income and an activity I enjoyed, as using creativity in my fashion came second nature to me. **Result:** I started independently modeling at twenty-one and eventually got signed to a reputable agency.

5. Vision: I've always liked running, playing tennis, and doing other physical activities. I had run a few half-marathons here and there but never committed to a full marathon. **Result:** The day I heard about the local run, I signed up and started my training soon after. Though my first marathon was no breeze, I kept at it and improved my abilities and outcome.

6. Vision: I've always wanted to be the best in anything and everything I came across. With sales being involved in every area of my life, I decided to become the top sales rep in the industry I once worked in. **Result:** I became just that. I became not only the top sales rep in the office but the top rep in the entire company, at one company after another—all employing several hundred to thousand reps.

I could go on and on and on. But just in case you haven't gotten the idea and the pattern here, it all boils down to this

powerful word called *intention.* Once we make the conscious
choice with ourselves and seriously commit to our decision, the rest becomes the history we choose to create for our older selves.

Moral of the story? You CAN have anything and everything you want in this abundant world. As soon as you start to truly practice self-development, LOA, a calm state of meditation, confidence, and a pure heart, any goal or dream you aspire to achieve one day will be yours.

You know, life is pretty simple. We all want the same things, especially things that make us feel good. We all want to use our youthful years to build something we believe in, grow it to the point where it affords us the lavish lifestyles we want, grow and build a family with someone we align with, have great health, travel the world, be happy, live a worthwhile life, have a handsome bank account we can rely on in our senior years (here come the discounts), and still have a generous amount left over for our families to enjoy. It's how we manifest those desires that makes the difference.

How can you practice self-development and the Law of Attraction today to begin living an abundant and prosperous life?

2 "Bruce Lee Be as Water My Friend," Terry Lee McBride, August 14, 2013, https://www.youtube.com/watch?v=cJMwBwFj5nQ.

CHAPTER 3: **STREET LAWYER**

You can have all the degrees in the world but if you don't have a hustler's mentality, ambition, and common sense, you'll be lost. -Nadia Buari

If you were honest with yourself, what would you say you have more of—book smarts or street smarts? Some people will automatically jump for book smarts and may be too afraid to admit that having street smarts is a good thing, reverting to the old-school limiting thoughts they were once told would serve them. Others will be honest with themselves and admit that, yes, they are somewhat more street smart than they are book smart.

Sure, being book smart has its perks. You get to have an experience of a lifetime, make great connections, and become an expert in a desired field. The cons? I know them all too well. You won't learn everything from just one or two books, especially if you don't apply the principles to your life. Aside from adding to your debt load and submitting to at least some level of brainwashing, going to school certainly has its perks.

On the other hand, being street smart can have its advantages as well. While the phrase "street smart" may bring up images of drug dealers and the like, the reality is many people end up on the streets for a variety of reasons. If we curb our assumptions and judgments to take a step back and consider all of the life- long lessons one can learn from such experiences, we may just find ourselves learning from people and places we never expected. Not only can street smarts help you navigate the world with a variety of people and their personalities, it can also allow you to get your way in the daily interactions and transactions we modern humans face. As they say, some things are meant to be learned through personal experience.

Why can't we be both street and book smart? By all means, keep pursuing the school knowledge, but take every opportunity to get more experience under your belt. Go back to school and pursue a higher degree in your field or educate yourself without the added debt by investing in books, seminars, events, and mentors who will teach you from their experience how to become good at the desired skill you wish to attain.

In terms of sales, the idea isn't to just get the book smarts and pay for all these resources just for the sake of becoming good at that one skill; the most important thing is being able to apply what you learn. There are so many people out there who would love to give you their two cents about any possible topic. They may even do whatever it takes to convince you that what they're saying is the be-all and end-all. But don't take their word for it. This is where the street smarts come in.

Be discerning. Use your critical-thinking skills. Take what's helpful and leave the rest. So when it comes to anything in life, especially the advice of others, you always want to take it with a grain of salt.

In the end, you need a filter or a plan. Don't just take in any and every piece of advice as if it were god-sent. Apply that same frame of mind to your transactions with others.

How can being both book smart and street smart contribute to your sales success today?

CHAPTER 4: **MINDSET**

Thoughts are the greatest vehicle to change, power, and success in the world. Everything begins with a thought-Oprah

What is the first thing that pops into your head when you think of the word *mindset*? I consider mindset to be a pattern of thinking and emotions that we've chosen to make up our human identities. It's pretty much the accumulation of everything that impacts us, the voices we allow to influence us in the deepest parts of ourselves.

In sales, this has serious implications for how we connect with our clients. Imagine a person who allows themselves to be influenced by and find pleasure in celebrity gossip. This person is absolutely obsessed with drama. Well, choosing to focus on drama is likely to lead him to a negative attitude, hence a poor mindset. This contributes to a pattern of not caring about anything that he *allows* to *happen to him*. Therefore, he feels his power has been given away and he's just a victim to everything that happens in his life. Such negative patterns of thought and a mindset of lack leads to more poor outcomes.

On the other hand, imagine people who choose to invest their time into educating themselves on the daily, staying up to date on the most mental, emotional, and physically health conscious research and materials—especially in regard to their professional lives. They choose to associate only with those who are always working on themselves and raising the bar on what society wants to call the norm. Rather than looking at the cup half empty, they see it half full. As a result, they are more inclined to pick up on positive and growth-related thinking only. That's what they find to be attractive; therefore, it will become their mindset.

Again, our mindset is really just an accumulation of the external forces we allow to influence us and the corresponding effects to our internal thoughts and emotions. Now if the influencers we chose had such a profound impact on our mindset, wouldn't you think the same would apply to what we call love? Of course it does! The type of person you *choose* to find attractive is dependent on the data you've accumulated from outside influences. I hope you know by now that most of our friends are like us because they validate our actions. In the same way, we are more inclined to attract a romantic partner who validates our choices. So if we choose to have a poor mindset, we are more inclined to find someone that reciprocates it. So, choose wisely.

Let's take it a step further. In the same way that our mindset makes us prone to attract certain friends and certain romantic partners, we can even attract a certain type of money and/or deal as well. When you go into a sales call thinking, *This is gonna go horribly. He'll never buy*, that's exactly what you attract from the client. Don't be surprised if he can't make a move for the life of him. Whereas, if you were to go into the call thinking *This will go great. John's not only gonna close on our top package at full price, but he will give me a solid referral as well*, that is what you will attract and manifest into your call.

You may be thinking, Now, of course, it's not that easy to be positive, right? I beg to differ. Nothing in life is ever easy without discipline. Just because something is not easy, doesn't mean you just throw your hands up and give in to a negative thought. In the same way that it takes time, practice, and dedication to become a negative person with a poor mindset, it takes that same type of repetition in the positive direction to have an abundant, positive, and fruitful mindset. Embrace the power of just one positive thought. Then watch how it can direct your outcome.

What will you do today to improve your mindset?

CHAPTER 5: **LISTENING > SPEAKING**

What we know is a drop, what we don't know is an ocean-Isaac Newton

You mean even during a sales meeting? That's right! Glad you're picking up so quickly! So here's the thing with silence. It can never be a bad thing, especially when it comes to sales. Whether you're waiting for a second or two to pass between the client's question and your answer, or you just dropped some gold and need to go silent so it could resonate with the client, silence is powerful. Silence speaks truth. I say that because with silence comes the simplicity of uncovering the truth of the sales rep, the client, and the truth from the sale.

I can't begin to explain how many times a client has at first felt awkward from my silence after I brought some value and positive insight to their business concern. Their response? "You're right, Bauer. Yeah, I didn't think of that before. Hmm, good point, Bauer."

My favorite is the situation when both the client and I go silent. A full minute may go by, and I'll ask, "Hey, Sara, you still there?" I'll immediately hear back, "Oh no no, I'm here, Bauer. I was just taking a minute to really hear what you're saying. Okay, well, how do I get started?"

Of course, that's exactly the result I will manifest. From hours and hours of brainwashing my mind with positive affirmations and self-development material and focusing ONLY on the outcome I want and WILL manifest, end results like that aren't just nice, they're expected. Remember, being a top-performing sales professional MUST include an expectation of ONLY excellence and a champion mindset like no other.

When you start to become more conscious toward the internal work you're striving to improve, you will naturally find the beauty in silence. As a result of becoming more conscious, you will soon become more aware of the energies you pick up from others. From just that one skill, you will know when and how to speak. Energy is unspeakable. It only comes to life when we have an open ear for it.

We find truth in the silence. And from that silence comes the right words in the right time. When you allow the silence to create space, you'll be amazed at how the words come naturally. But ONLY when you allow them in.

What can you do today to be more conscious of the words you choose and listen more intently to your clients?

CHAPTER 6: **T.R.U.T.H.**

Truth exists; only lies are invented-Georges Braque

What is the truth? When it comes to this topic or that, how can we rely on what we believe to be true? As we discussed in previous chapters, our truth is determined by what and who we *choose* to be influenced by. This, of course, boils down to what we *want* to believe as well. We as a human race tend to believe whatever validates us, our decisions, and/or beliefs.

There's risk involved in this approach. Whenever we make the decision (hopefully, it's a conscious one) to believe what we're told, we cancel out the possibilities of what's out there, a potentially more defined truth. Our future is strictly dependent on the decisions we choose to make in the now and those we've made in the past. So the next time you are presented with information, question its truth, and ask yourself if it matches up with your conscious truth (no egos or insecurities allowed).

When we apply this frame of thinking toward sales, we can start to break down all the different functions that come along with it. Whether it's a belief held by your client, your colleague, or even yourself.

The key is to constantly (humbly) question whatever claim you're presented with. Now, remember, the goal isn't to disagree with something and argue with everyone you come into contact with. The motive here is to help yourself and those in your path find truth—both individually and as a group.

Your *approach* to confronting false or incomplete information is key. Most clients are used to having random information thrown at them. Make sure that what you share with clients comes from a humble place and that your only goal is to be in tune with your client, to reach the same positive frequency. Trust me, there's no better feeling than knowing you've earned your client's trust. The reverse is true, too—a client is overjoyed to find they trust a salesperson's judgment and motives.

Be conscious in the moment and ask yourself what your truth really is and what that means to you, as well as those around you.

How will you find truth in your professional dealings, and how will that change the way you live?

CHAPTER 7: **VAL-YOU-E**

Price is what you pay. Value is what you get-Warren Buffett

When it comes to our professional lives, most of us know all too well how powerfully and beneficially value serves our business. Below is a scenario that helps explain this theory of value over price. The key is to sell a product based on the value it brings to your client instead of the price of your product.

Seller's side: Let's say our sales representative, Bauer, represents a marketing company that provides a few great features to clients in the restaurant business. These features may include campaigns across social media, promotional TV ads, and a partnership with the local grocery store. She has a prospect she's been working with for quite some time, and she finally schedules a follow-up meeting with the sole owner to discuss the last-minute details, and hopefully, get his signature for a six-month agreement from him. Let's call him Pete.

Bauer shows up for the meeting, and within a few minutes of speaking with Pete, she realizes that this business owner is really afraid of signing up—mainly because he's been burned in the past. She waits a few seconds after Pete unconsciously spills his fears and proceeds with a strategic go-to. Firstly, she levels with Pete and tells him that his hesitations are all too common among first-time buyers.

In a very respectful, calm, confident, and conscious manner, Bauer follows that with one value proposition after another. Now, she's not just dumping every one of the company's value props on Pete. Remember, she doesn't want to overwhelm him with information that he's not ready for. Instead, she provides him straight data and numbers that prove the validity and quality of the product and/or service.

By providing relevant data to Pete's concerns, she's able to not only gain his trust but also his full attention. Using logic and business acumen, Bauer is able to earn the business at full price. Bauer walks away a happy business consultant, and Pete, a happy customer.

Buyer's side: Now let's look at the same scenario from Pete's perspective. Pete represents a family-owned restaurant. The business was passed down from his great-grandfather to his grandfather. Pete's grandfather passed the business down to Pete's father, and after thirty years of operation, the business just recently became Pete's possession and responsibility. Being that he's only had it for the past ten years, he's noticed a steady number of current and loyal customers coming in consistently. However, he finds that it's been nearly impossible for him to get new customers in; the lunch rush isn't even worth it. He has tried multiple marketing programs before, but nothing seems to really bring in results.

After speaking to Bauer and learning more about what her company can offer, he admitted to himself and even his wife (whom he runs ideas by) that he seriously wants to consider doing business with Bauer. Pete found himself doing hours and hours of research between the day of their meeting and their follow-up meeting a week later. From all of his research, he couldn't find any reason not to give Bauer's program a try. However, he just kept reverting back to his fear of losing money, as that's been the result of every other program he's tried in the past. He eventually talked himself out of the sale and was convinced that when he spoke to Bauer again, he was not going to purchase her program.

However, when he speaks to Bauer, he feels that his concerns are heard, respected, and taken into consideration. He feels that Bauer really cares about his business and what it represented to his customers. Pete loves how Bauer doesn't come across as being pushy. In fact, her tone is more consultative than anything. After thinking it through some more, he decides that her company is the most logical move for his business and that he should give it a try. He feels great about his purchase and puts only positive thoughts behind his decision.

As you can see from this example, it's not about being pushy or judging others when it comes to business transactions. Simply put, we're people dealing with other people, and once we can get the other person to like us and feel respected, heard, and cared for, we're golden (on both ends).

Some common prospect objections to love (never to fear): Budget—give value.

The customer will find the money; whether they take out a loan for it, trade for it, or allocate funds differently. Ask them what/who they are comparing your company to. Use a story related to something they like to buy.

Shoes, for example: "Let's say you went into your favorite department store and found an amazing pair of shoes that you couldn't walk away from. You look into your bank account and realize you have to transfer money from your savings into your checking account, ask if you can open a store credit card, or even try to pull the good ole Kevin Hart—"You see, the way my bank account is set up ..." (Get them to laugh.) "At the end of the day, you love those shoes. No matter what you have to do, you will find a way to buy them, right? Well then, Pete, either I didn't show you enough to make your decision today, or there's something else you're not telling me." Case closed.

Time—give value.

Ask them when they want to launch this in front of their clients. Ask when they want their staff/partners to be familiar with it. Ask: "Why not now? What's the difference between now and [name a moment in the future]?"

The only time this is not an excuse and is a valid objection is when we're talking businesses being sold, facing foreclosures, or any other legal issue that might affect the sale. What's a better time? Have them explain their logical reasoning behind it.

Personal Issues—give value.

How can they use this opportunity to set themselves apart from their competition? How can your company ease this positive transition for them? Work with them here.

Scared of change—give value.

Gently reinforce that change is an inevitable part of life and business. If they don't change, it's hard to say they'll ever grow. How else can they stay on top of their competition?

Does any of this sound familiar? By focusing on the value you can bring to your clients, you change your entire sales game around. Use it wisely.

How much of a difference would you make in your sales today if you start focusing on value in your consultations?

CHAPTER 8: **FAITH OR FEAR**

Fear is not real. It is a product of thoughts you create. Do not misunderstand me. Danger is very real. But fear is a choice-Will Smith

No matter what industry you sell in or where in the world you may be reading this book, one piece of advice applies across the board: don't show all your cards.

Let's say you're in a sales meeting and the client is asking for a deal on your product. The more value you give them, the more they keep agreeing with it but saying they have to stick to their $20 when your lowest product is $200. *SMH* Trust me, this scenario is all too common.

Now, instead of throwing out a discount here and there, the best solution would be to start sharing your value props with success stories or help them imagine what good would come to their business by *investing,* not just *spending* on what you're trying to sell them.

Once you can help the prospect overcome this mindset hump and get them to start thinking along the lines of the countless possibilities you can bring to their business, you're golden. No need for any discount at that point. Why? You have given so much value and insight into the meeting that the client not only buys your product but states that your product "is the Mercedes Benz of (the industry that you serve)." I'm speaking strictly from experience here.

The power of influence is extremely important. Who you listen to determines your checks. Yes, it's 100% possible to take a bad lead and turn it into that top package gold platter you'll be served later that night for dinner. You determine the client's view on the business you represent. Your style of persuasiveness and tonality, the stories you tell, and the humble persistence you show will get you there, NOT those discounts you've been offering left or right.

Discounting not only devalues your product—it devalues you as a representative of the product. So next time a client tries to push you into giving them a discount, drop these gems and, worst-case scenario, ask them about something they really like.

Showcase your product. Make it the star. It's the best in your industry, just as you are the best salesperson to represent this product to them. *Humbly* act as if you're the best [insert your title] in the company you represent. That demeanor itself will be very obvious to the client. They will pick up on it.

With these clever strategies comes the skill to sell anything to anyone in such a witty manner that even the client can't notice or be "bothered" by handing over that credit card.

What will you say today to the client who says he/she can't afford your product?

CHAPTER 9: **SHARE THE POSITIVITY**

It takes both sides to build a bridge-Fredrik Nael

Ever seen a really great movie where the producer did such an amazing job portraying the story that you get emotionally involved all the way to its happy ending? Of course you have. Even if, like me, you're not a big movie-watcher, I'm sure you've seen one or two before that had an impact on you.

The same principle applies in sales. Now, for those clients we all love so much, let's figure out how we can cash in those sales. How can we use storytelling to have that same impact on our "tough" clients?

Whether we're dealing with a client who's afraid to take the first step in the marketing success of their business to a client who's been burned time and time again by countless false-hope programs he's purchased, there's a story for each and every single one of them.

Let's say you come across a client who you feel may benefit from another's experience, but you don't have a relatable story ready to share. No problem! Go to the top rep in the company and ask for some great success stories and pick one that relates most to the client you're "struggling" to close.

Sharing a story with a client is important and healthy for the sale to process through, but sincerity is a must. By that I mean you should be honest with your clients. Honesty not only makes a great impression on your client's experience, but it's good karma that will soon pay off in the form of some solid referrals— where you can double, triple, or even quadruple that commission check. I'm speaking from experience here. Being a sales professional is about more than just the sale you're facing directly; it's also about those that will trickle down to you before that commission check hits your bank account.

What stories will you start sharing in your sales meeting today?

CHAPTER 10: **CHECKS, PLEASE!**

Patience is bitter, but its fruit is sweet-Aristotle

Now let's talk about all those Lengthy Larry's you may have somewhere in the pipeline. I once had a Larry I will never forget. Larry had come to me with a serious business issue he was having, but no matter how much value I provided him, he refused to make the move. This took place in the early half of the first quarter. I catered my demo specifically toward his business needs, gave him success stories, and even provided phone numbers to my current clients that do similar work.

Every month, I'd set aside time in my calendar to give Larry a ring and check in on him. Yes, there were many calls that he didn't answer, *despite how many different ways I went about it.* Larry was just an interesting man. I called, emailed, texted—I tried anything I could think of to get him back on the phone. I even went as far as sending him a handwritten letter to catch his attention, but he was a no-go.

Despite how closed off Larry had become, I didn't give up on him for the simple reason that I knew the value I could bring to his business. I was confident that my product could change his business for the better. So as the months went by, I continued to reach out every so often but made sure that, despite all my attempts, I wasn't being too pushy,   just persistent.

There's a major difference there. Persistence is the tenacity to never give up on a goal. Now, by goal, I mean something you strive for that's moral, ethical, and in the best interest of all parties involved. Amateurs *only* focus on what they'll get from the sale, but professionals have an eye for how both they *and* their client will benefit. Which are you? Are you curious about how my multiple conversations with Larry went?

February

Me: Hey, Larry. It's Bauer. How's it going?! (I make it a point to ALWAYS be enthusiastic.)

Larry: Oh, hey, Bauer. Good. You?

Before I could say anything, Larry hung up.

I smiled, left my notes in the CRM I was using, and moved on to the next call. Was I giving up? Heck no! This happened on multiple occasions during the following weeks.

March

Me: Hey, Larry! How's it going? Larry: Who's this? It's Bauer with—

Seconds later, Lare Bear hung up again. This time I sent him a very nice "hang up" text template I came up with. This was Phase One: friendly reminder time. Something along the lines of:

"Hey, Larry, it's Bauer with [insert company name]. I'm not sure what exactly happened there, but the call ended abruptly. When would be a better time for us to reconnect?"

He never responded, so I put him on an email campaign I came up with.

April

Me: Hey, Larry. It's Bauer. How's it going? (I acted as if the previous calls never took place.)

Larry: Oh, hey, Bauer. I'm well, thanks. Hold on a sec, would you?

Guess what happened this time? Larry hung up again, ha! Phase Two: call

him out.

Me via Text: Hey, Larry. It's Bauer. So, oddly enough, once we started our conversation, the call suddenly ended. Now, whether it was intentional or not, please do me a favor and let me know if you're seriously interested in skyrocketing your business with the top ... in the ... industry. We look forward to hearing from you. :) (I use the smile at the end to lighten up the energy of the text).

Larry: Yes, Bauer. How about tomorrow at 1 p.m.

Me: 1 p.m. sounds great, Larry. Look out for a calendar invite from me.

I sent him a ten-minute (only) calendar invite. The idea behind this is to make sure Larry understands I respect my time as much as his. That way he's more inclined to show up, being it's an agreed-upon time.

The day came, and Larry showed up for the call. He asked for a recap on the original conversation we had four months earlier. I went over it with him once more, and he started to bring up the timing objection. We went back and forth, but nothing seemed to resonate with Larry, so we agreed to touch base and set a solid close date.

Month after month, Larry kept pushing off his signup date. He refused to answer his phone for quite some time. Finally, I got him on a call in mid-July.

July

A few hours before the scheduled calendar meeting, I texted him my "follow-up template."

Me: Hi, Larry. It's Bauer. I look forward to our call today. We will go over the package that you want to move forward with. You'll sign the contract, and ... (This way, I let Larry know what's about to go down when we get on the call). So, Larry, I know you and I have gone back and forth for some time now, but I'm confident in your decision. Now, which package were you looking to get started with today?

Larry: Um, yeah, can we talk about your top package?

Me: Yes. So, what you'll get is ...

After dropping in more value, I finally got Larry's agreement on the deal, and I completed the transaction. Larry admitted the following.

Larry: You know, Bauer, I really appreciate you reaching out and staying persistent with me. Without you, I don't think I'd ever have agreed on this program or any program for that matter!

Me: Haha! Thank you, Larry. I knew you would eventually. Glad we were able to get you started with us.

Larry: Yes. And also, Bauer, I'm very sorry for the things I said and all the times I hung up on you. You've honestly been great, and I must say I'm very impressed with your sales approach to the point that I'd like to extend an offer to you.

Silence is key here.

Larry: I'd like to offer you a position within my company as the head of sales. Do you happen to have a personal email where I can send you some information?

Me: Larry, thank you very much for the offer. I'm truly honored, but I must stay true to my calling and the company I currently represent.

Larry: I understand, Bauer. Well, hey, if you ever change your mind, you know how to reach me!

Me: Haha. I sure do, Larry. Well, hey, let me be the first to welcome you to the ... family! I look forward to hearing about your business success and to getting some referrals from you! :)

Larry: Absolutely, Bauer. Thank you!

There you go. Not only does persistence get you a solid deal in the end, but it also widens your potential for some referrals and an additional form of income.

What will you do today to be persistent with a Lengthy Larry in your pipeline?

CHAPTER 11: **RELATE WITH KINDNESS**

The best marketing strategy ever: care-Gary Vaynerchuk

We live in a world where relating to and connecting with other human beings is essential to our well-being. Since that's the case, we have to admit one truth that will change our whole perspective on sales. No matter what industry you're in— medical, marketing, restaurant, beauty, transportation, etc.—we are ALL in the people industry.

Like it or not, we all have to deal with people on a daily basis. Just because we're not *in the office* doesn't mean we're not still *on the job*. Sales and transactions are always going on around us. The store clerk is checking out the customer. The banker is talking about loans to the customer seated in his office. The nail tech wants us to get a mani AND a pedi! The school advisor is encouraging the student to sign up for an advanced class. Do we consider those sales or just people *doing their job*?

It's as simple as this: the thought we give to the act of selling. Once you can successfully believe you are bringing a service or product of value to the table, both you and your clients will benefit from the sale. Believe it or not, your clients can always read the thoughts you unconsciously wear all over your face. Body language and mannerisms speak louder than words—even on that sales call. What we think and portray is what our clients take in and act upon. You can either attract a positive transaction or a negative one.

So next time you find it difficult to get your client to open up and engage with you during your sales presentation, try connecting with them and relating to them on a personal level. Whether you talk about sports, family, a national holiday, or weekend plans, anything will help. Of course, keep it appropriate and moral here. Don't bring up religion, politics, or anything that could potentially hinder that sale you're working toward. Be flexible and relatable; be a chameleon.

Now if you're really just in sales for the sake of "having a job" and loving the commission lifestyle, let's talk. When you don't genuinely care about your clients' success and the impact your product is having on them, please do yourself a favor and find a product and/or company that you do believe in. Can you fake it, till you make it? Of course. Anyone can! But this book isn't about how you can make a quick buck. I'm here to tell you that dollar of yours will go much further when you can sell something you believe in, invest in, and even spend your hard-earned dollars on! You'll get much further. Trust me on this one.

How would your sales meetings improve today if you were to start relating to your client on a more personal and genuine level?

CHAPTER 12: **REVERSE THAT RETURN**

Rule No. 1: Never lose money.

Rule No. 2: Don't forget rule No. 1-Warren Buffett

In regard to reversing a return, we must first understand ROI. You'd be surprised how many business owners I've come across have no clue what ROI stands for, let alone what it is and the impact it could have on their business.

Let's break it down very simply here. ROI stands for *return on investment*. In other words, when you invest X amount of money into a deal, business, or program—anything you choose to view as an investment, as opposed to just another overhead cost— you want to know how much you'll take home from that investment, right? The following scenario explains this strategy in more detail. You'll love this one.

Seller's side: Mel is an esthetician and gets approached by a website developing and promoting company offering her a once-in-a-lifetime deal, which she's always been curious about. She goes through the demonstration with Bauer, one of the company's top sales representatives, and loves what they do, but she's immediately frightened. She's always been drawn to the idea of signing up but doesn't want to pay until she gets a client. However, Bauer's solution doesn't offer that type of payment system. Mel would have to pay the day she signs up; of course, it would be a prorated cost for the remainder of the month. Her first full payment wouldn't be due until the first of the following month.

After they've exchanged a few emails, Mel decides to go dark on Bauer. She doesn't answer any of her emails or calls. However, about a month goes by, lo and behold, Bauer gets an inbound call from Mel. She asks Bauer to revisit their program and the cost once again. She asks for a discount, and Bauer kindly responds that there are none available. She goes on to offer some value content to catch Mel's attention and maybe even calm her nerves. Bauer can tell Mel is very concerned and worried. However, that doesn't seem to do much for her.

Then Bauer goes for the reverse ROI method. Bauer finds out that with the program Mel is currently subscribed to, she gets about two facials a week (eight facials a month). Her average facial typically costs up to $100 an hour; however, the program she goes through takes half of the proceeds from each client they send her. So despite not paying anything up front, Mel spends nearly $400 a month with her current company. Not only that. She hasn't gotten much return from any of these discount customers she's been attracting.

Bauer explains again how her company's solution would only cost Mel a fraction of that price *and* offer her full-price customers, website promoting, and a solid retention number she can show her investor, whom she meets with on a quarterly basis.

Long story short, Bauer cashes in the deal, and Mel walks away a happy and more conscious business owner.

Buyer's side: Mel has found her numbers are continuing to drop month after month; she's seeing a decrease in customer acquisition. She puts in an online request to speak with Bauer's company, but soon she finds herself feeling overwhelmed and fearful. Without Bauer saying or doing a thing, she feels that she needs to take her time in making a decision regarding her business concerns. She goes on doing the same thing, week after week, praying for better results. She soon comes to the realization that she should probably give Bauer's company a shot, but she really dislikes the idea of having to pay upfront without first seeing results. Out of the blue one Monday afternoon, she gives Bauer a ring and asks to go over her solution and prices. Bauer does so and explains how they do not offer discounts with their program, considering its excellent success rate in Mel's local area.

Bauer helps Mel break down how much she's spending a month with her current provider. Once Bauer helps her reevaluate her perception toward spending money, Mel soon opens her mind to the possibility of results awaiting her. She agrees with Bauer's way of thinking and soon finds herself signing up for the program.

Months go by, and Mel not only gives Bauer's company a great five-star review online, she even refers one of her close friends to the same program. She ends up doubling her sales and does so by raking in the full price and loyal customers she'd been dreaming of all along.

The moral of the story is we can't force people who may not "get it" to see as we do. That simply doesn't work. But by being a genuine human being, you can prove your point by providing logic and care to your prospects and soon-to- be loyal and long-term customers.

What will you do today to improve on your—and your client's—ROI?

CHAPTER 13: **MANIFEST YOUR DREAM CLIENT**

Stop focusing on dumb things-Gary Vaynerchuk

Now I'm sure many of us, at some point in our sales career, have complained about a client being this or that. But as they say, the truth will set you free. NEVER, ever blame your client for your lack of skill in closing them. Of course, there are situations out there that may prevent a client from closing— such as a closed business, a foreclosure, a change of career, the passing of a loved one, etc. Those are things we can never change—nor should we even consider it. Those factors are completely out of our control. The only response in that case is to send our condolences and/or give a positive solution in the near future, and only when the client is ready for the transaction. Sending a handwritten card in the meantime would go a long way too. Trust me on this one. I've experienced this on several occasions. But know one thing: you should ONLY focus on what you can control.

Now that's out of the way, let's talk about how you can focus on attracting the right clients into your pipeline.

Consider the list of ideal client attributes below:

Mindset: abundant

Attitude: positive and naturally inquisitive

Time line: ASAP

Budget: flexible

Decision-maker: SSP (Single Service Provider) and/or just the person I'm working with

Decision-making process: on the spot up to 24-hour follow-up (case by case)

Pain points: great match to the solution we offer Familiarity w/ spending money: very Respectful: very

Professional: very

Change: adaptable

Risk: loves it

Referrals: yes, very referral-friendly

As you can see, my ideal client is not impossible. I've attracted a version of this time and time again. Yes, there have been some exceptions here and there, but this is the type of client I focus on attracting most.

Do yourself a favor and come up with your ideal client. List their attributes on your computer or a piece of paper. Save it on your desktop or even as the screensaver on your cell phone. That way it's ALWAYS top of mind. This can be someone you wish you could speak to on a regular basis, do business with, and want that "type" of client to be your new norm. When you focus on the type of client you want to work with, you'll attract them time after time.

What will you do today to manifest your dream client?

CHAPTER 14: **DO WE MATCH?**

The human connection is the key to personal and career success-Paul J. Meyer

Manifesting your dream clients is an important and powerful exercise, and it will generate amazing results. However, we still live in the real world, and there are times we'll encounter clients who aren't an ideal match. It's just a fact of life that we'll occasionally have clients we don't naturally connect with. Are those cases a lost cause?

No, of course not. They are *opportunities* to meet our clients where they are. Let's explore some practical ways to do that.Imagine a great couple. One partner complements the other, right? The same is true of your relationship with a client. Of course, we're talking about keeping it appropriate here and being in tune with the other party. Let's face it: without a client, there won't be a sales rep with a product for him or her to buy.

Let's talk about the connection we need in a sales transaction. In order to get a strong connection to the client, it's important to optimize your communication style with the client.

First comes the tone. As I like to say, this is the music to the attitude the sales professional chooses to have that day. Of course, I can't share an example of tonality with you here in this book. But I can certainly do it through syntax, right? By carefully choosing the right words to describe your product or how you feel about its value to your business, you can portray the tone that's the best fit.

The next aspect to be conscious of is the speed of your words. Have you ever considered matching the client's speed? Good idea! That's exactly what I'm getting at here. This helps the client feel like you're both in it together—on the same page, at the same pace—which helps them trust you and speak more freely. Vocabulary is next. Whether your client has a more elementary vocabulary or uses big words left and right, the key is to match them. If their word choice intimidates you and you simply don't understand a word or two they're using, take a few milliseconds and look up the words online as the client is still speaking. Or just embrace humility and ask them to elaborate on what they mean by a word or phrase you don't understand.

Whether we're speaking about tonality, speed, or desired syntax, our main motive stays the same: to connect with the client and *help* them break down their limiting anti-salespeople beliefs. The more you can do that successfully, the fewer clients you'll have who "just don't get it." Remember, it's never the client's fault that they didn't buy. Closing the sale is on us.

By putting the control and focus on yourself (the only person you *can* or should control), you take control of the commission that comes your way.

What will you do today to start connecting with and matching your clients more closely?

CHAPTER 15: **TIME > MONEY**

My favorite things in life don't cost any money. It's really clear that the most precious resource we all have is time. -Steve Jobs

Money, money, money. Or should it be time, time, time? Well, what's more important? Ask yourself that question. On a short-term versus long-term basis, what's more important?

For some people, time may equal money. For others, money may be the priority. How you answer the question determines your success and the kind of life you build for yourself.

Now, what we do with the time we have determines the success our future holds- Yours Truly, Bauer Doski

Consider the following scenario as an exploration of how we prioritize time and money. **Seller's Side:** Tom, a frustrated owner of an Italian restaurant, calls Bauer regarding their online marketing campaigns. She runs him through a full demonstration of both her product and services. Tom goes from being super interested and engaged during the sales call to being on the defense. Now being the successful salesperson that Bauer is, she's already brought up pricing at the start of the call, and Tom has agreed that it was in his budget.

They go back and forth. At first, Tom says he's good; he's no longer interested. But through Bauer's patient conversation,

Tom switches sides, saying he likes the program. Instead of matching Tom's anxious energy and tone, Bauer brings him back to square one and reminds him why he was interested in the first place by asking him specific questions that get him to give her what she wants to hear.

After she calmly brings up his pain points and the reason for his initial call, she simply connects each pain point to a solution (features her company offers). Bauer shows enthusiasm, care, and true respect for Tom's business concerns.
After she's done making her solid point, she puts the ball in his court and starts talking numbers.

Bauer: *Now please tell me, Tom. When you bring up your current solution, how much of a return are you currently getting?*
Tom: *Well ... I haven't really looked into that yet. I just know I pay a guy to stand out on the corner to hold up a street sign for eight hours Monday through Friday. I only pay him $9 an hour! He's the most loyal employee I've got!*
Bauer: *Okay, so from the eight hours that your employee is standing outside, how many clients is he getting off the road and into the shop, on average?*
Tom: *About four a month?*

Bauer: Geez, so now I know why we've been talking. Okay, so let's break it down here. You said earlier that your average meal costs about $12– $14, correct?

Tom: Yes, it does.

Bauer: So, after taxes, you pay him roughly $800 a month, give or take. From the $1,440 you pay him (before taxes), he generates about $56 a month in return.

In order to emphasize her point, Bauer goes silent. **Get comfortable with silence.**

Tom: Yeah ... I mean, I guess that's right. He gets it. He's just a bit embarrassed.

Bauer: Do you need me to run those numbers by you again? You NEED to be on the same page as the client, ESPECIALLY when it comes to the numbers.

Tom: Oh no, no I get it.

Bauer: So you're currently spending about $1,384 (before taxes) per month. Let's talk about how we can do a better job of getting customers in your doors at a lower cost. And maybe we can get that loyal employee of yours inside the restaurant waiting tables on all the customers we'll get you? She says this in a humorous tone to lighten the mood.

Tom: Bauer, you're right. Let's get started. How do I sign up? Do you take visa?

Customer's Side: Okay, so we have Tom, frustrated and upset over his business decisions. He feels that his employee outside is the most loyal he has, so he doesn't want to let him go. He can't seem to get many customers in his doors and will do whatever it takes to get that taken care of. A friend of his recommends Bauer's company and tells him how much they've helped generate for his wife's business.

Tom ponders this for a few weeks and finally makes the call. After going over the program, he gets cold feet and tries to talk himself out of it. Bauer helps to reassure him of his decision and helps him see a logical breakdown of his costs. She gives him an alternative in signing up for a proven program that's helped almost every other small business in his area *and* shows him a way to promote that loyal employee of his.

Though Tom signs up, he still feels a bit afraid of the outcome. Bauer shares one of her client success stories to help calm his nerves. He finishes his term with the company and calls Bauer six months later to sign up for another.

I hope you see that time is more valuable than money. You can always get possession of money. You can earn it, loan it, or even trade for it. But time— that's something you can never get back. Now, as far as your future time goes, you can put a strategy in place right now to save that before it's here.

What can you do today to save time and/or money?

CHAPTER 16: **FROM EXCELLENCE TO REFERRAL$**

People influence people. Nothing influences people more than a recommendation from a trusted friend ... A trusted referral is the Holy Grail of advertising-Mark Zuckerberg

Active Referrals

Being that we're on the topic of referrals, let's talk about how to manifest that positive cash flow. Let's say you complete a killer demonstration of your product, and your client loves it so much they decide to go with your top package. You talk about it for days and start to walk around the office like a big shot, right?

No. Let's go about this humbly. Let's close the deal like a boss. We get the client excited and ready to sign up for our top package, and we send them a handwritten card with a few of our business cards inside the envelope. A week or two goes by, so we send a quick text or email their way to check in. Once we manifest and get that positive response, we give them a good old-fashion ring and ask for some referrals. In exchange, we offer a "special" incentive for them *in addition* to the success they've already experienced from the product we've signed them up under.

We call on the referral. This time, when we go through the product (if we have to), we don't have that much to prove or work toward because our good friend who initially closed, let's call him Dan, has already put in a stellar word for us. So cash in those referrals, baby!

Think about how many sales would chase you from all the referrals you could get from just that one original sale with Danny boy. Let's say Dan gives you four referrals that you easily close, and from each of those four, you get three or four more referrals. The rest is history.

From all my years in sales, I've learned this is one of the biggest areas where sales reps can easily cash in some extra sales —simply by running one badass demo.

Now don't take this the wrong way and say, "Oh, Bauer said to just run one outstanding demo and ..." No, that's not what I'm recommending.

Give your all, and I mean your ALL, to every opportunity that comes your way. Run the best demo of your life every single time, and best believe when you ask the universe/client to support you, success will be yours.

Passive referrals

With your direct sales gig to the side, let's talk about how to build passive income from the same approach: referrals. Being the smart reader you are, I'm sure you know the difference between passive and active income, right? Good. So how do you manifest income with just one transaction?

First and foremost, tap into more than one market. Don't just sell in one and only one industry. Find something you're good at and create a badass product or self-paying service out of it. From there, find a way to promote your work where your job is done.

I'll give you a quick example from my own life. I got into the art of modeling in my twenties. I found a way to get signed to an agency *and* get paid gigs (always asking for equity). I *also* found a way to sell my work. So not only would I get compensation for the gig, but I also had equity and a percentage of sales adding up in my bank account. In addition to that, I had my work on ecommerce platforms and had previous groups refer me as talent.

Apart from the initial setup work, no extra effort was required on my end. From there came the referrals of my work, without me doing any promoting. Again, a little work in the short-term for much long-term gain.

Never apply all of your sales skills in just one industry. Always strive to generate multiple streams of sales income. Always be closing in any field you find value in. Always be closing. Until it becomes second nature. Until you could do it in your sleep.

How would your commission check(s) increase today if you were to start implementing a referral program of your skills?

CHAPTER 17: **WHERE TO?**

Look forward, that's where you're going-Unknown

Have you ever been in a sales meeting, a conference or on a call where you felt confused and couldn't retain what the client said or, worse, whether they would close? I hope you can respond no to that. So here's the thing with a successful sale—whether from a *one call close* or a few meetings in—you **ALWAYS, ALWAYS, ALWAYS** need a plan.

You NEVER want to leave a sales meeting without either a bank account and routing number, credit card, and/or a signed legal contract (which you should have multiple copies of) or a follow-up meeting to close on a future date. This gives both you and the client an organized framework for the next steps. This is also a great way to push the sale forward in an organized, professional and respectful manner.

Trust me, even for the most scattered clients I've encountered, this practice creates a positive outcome. Remember, with more risk comes more reward.

A solid plan for the future is helpful on many levels. And being future- oriented will maintain the health of your ever-evolving pipeline. So remember, always have a plan before you start anything. Here's an example of what your goals might look like before you pick up that phone and make another phone call or walk in for that introduction.

Introductory conversation: the goal is to either run your demonstration on the fly or schedule a date and time to do so.

Meeting day: the goal is to complete your demo and process the sale or to schedule a *solid* date and time at least 24–48 hours away from the original meeting.

Closing day: the goal is to close the deal and rake in those referrals.

Of course, this plan will differ from one industry and type of sale to another.

However, the motive is still the same: ALWAYS have a plan in place to move the sale forward.

What will you do today to continue moving the ball forward in your sales meetings?

CHAPTER 18: **THE POWER OF EXECUTION**

When you want to succeed as bad as you want to breathe-Eric Thomas

We've all heard it before: *Hard work pays off.* Hmm, well yes, but what does "hard work" mean to you? Just like any of the other topics we've covered, the definition that you choose to give *hard work* comes from your influences. How have other people in your life defined "hard work" for you?

Our adolescent years include social conditioning that we carry into our adult years. Not many of us will sit back and evaluate our thoughts, where they came from, whether they're good for us, and if we should yield to a more beneficial thought process.

So after you define what work ethic means to you, you can start the evaluation phase. This is where you have to be 100% honest with yourself. Do you leave the office feeling *fulfilled* and excited for the next day to come? Or do you leave the office feeling *relieved* to go home to vent?

Fulfillment—what does that word mean to you? Define this for yourself.

What about *anxiousness*? Define this term and recall how the emotion feels to you. You'll soon realize the two are polar opposites. One contradicts the other. You simply can't be one with the other, unless your mind is so scattered that you don't know what to feel or believe.

It's crucial that you're honest with yourself here. Your end results and degree of success are determined by your willingness to admit your areas of growth.

What level of discipline do you believe people like Gandhi, Buddha, and Mother Teresa brought to their lives and their work? Hyper-focused discipline—that's the level we're talking about here.

What are you failing to do that you *know* needs to change? In all my years of sales, I've seen one person after another easily admit what they need to change but refuse to put in the work and stand by their word. What ends up happening in that situation? They continue to leave work every single day feeling relieved to have ended the day and dreading the next.

I call such people *average sales representatives*. On the other end of the spectrum, you have the *fulfilled sales professionals*. These people are all too rare. The silver lining is that this leaves more money on the table for the ones who want it badly enough. These are the sales reps who start working before they even get to the office, put in a full workday and keep working after they leave—day in and day out. They may seem quiet and *laser-focused* on hitting their target number. They find pleasure and 100% commitment and fulfillment in the job.

Any overtime hours? Haha! Yes, these champions have a can-do and a whatever-it-takes attitude. It's no wonder a combination of these two, the fulfilled sales professional and the average sales representative, are found in every sales field. Which one do you want to be? The choice is yours.

What will you start doing today to improve your work ethic?

CHAPTER 19: **YOUR OMNIPOTENT ABILITIES**

At some point I had to stop asking—can I be great, can I be brilliant, can I be ok and still be accepted? I just stopped asking permission and just gave notice unapologetically-Lisa Nichols

Do you believe that you create both the good and the bad that comes into your life? Do you believe that you have full control of your experiences, where you've been and where you're going? Glad to hear we're on the same page here.

How do you feel about this idea of us all having omnipotent abilities over the outcomes of our lives? Whether you realize it or not, who you represent to yourself is who you present to others. What you think, feel, say, and do to yourself works exactly the same toward others. With that comes this powerful ability we all have to take full responsibility over anything and everything in our lives.

Now, of course, each of us come from our own cultural and religious background. I have the utmost respect for that. So please strive to be open- minded as you read the next few chapters. I hope you can interpret what I propose in a way that allows you to still have faith in a higher power. You can call it God, Source, the Universe, or anything else that resonates with you.

For those of us who are awake and fully aware of this omnipotent ability we possess, good job! Keep growing. For those who don't yet grasp the power within you, great! Keep growing.

The point here is that no matter where you are in your self-development journey, there will always be room for growth and improvement. It's within you to act upon what you learn, you have the power to become the conscious and fulfilled individual you strive to be. Being that we all create our existence, the existence of other humans, and everything else in this world of ours, would it be fair to say that we are the creators of our realities?

Of course we are! We not only create our lives and everything that exists around it, but we are all limitless. Whether or not we want to accept that, we will eventually come to this realization; trust me.

Now that we're on the same page, let's talk about the inner voice of our god-like presence: our intuition. As they say, *intuition will never lead you astray.* That's true. So if we're going to allow intuition to guide us in our relationships and other aspects of our lives, why not embrace and strengthen this power within us to guide our sales career as well?

What about the client who says he will buy but won't commit to a time and date? No matter how many ways you go about asking for the confirmed follow- up, you just can't seem to get it from him. Instead, you agree to a follow-up email and take things from there—knowing if you don't hear from him within the week, you will give him a call. (You keep this to yourself, of course, so he won't take his time throughout the week in making a decision.)

You get off the phone feeling as if you just agreed to something unfamiliar and somewhat risky. But you stick with your intuition. You go with your gut. Hours later, you get a call and he's ready to sign up!

I laugh at this success story every time I recall it. Not because it challenged and forced me to grow as a professional but because it was an opportunity for me to respect, trust, and build a stronger bond with my omnipotent power within.

Moral of the story, even if the client doesn't close or agree on something within your timeline, still give the demo your all, but don't cancel out the deal. In short: listen to your intuition.

How can you use the experiences from today to help you get closer to that limitless power within you?

CHAPTER 20: **WITH JUST NO MONEY DOWN!**

Long-term consistency trumps short-term intensity-Bruce Lee

So then comes this idea of no money down. Who does that naturally attract? Well, insecure and less confident buyers, of course! We've all been there—we wanted to purchase something but felt a bit hesitant to make a huge investment into this great idea or project we have. So we find someone who tells us it'll cost little to no money to get started; they promise to get us the same results that the #1 company can at a lower cost. Thinking short-term and not focusing much on the long-term effects, we go ahead and get started.

I mean what do we have to lose, right? Let's play this out with a real-life example.

Seller's Side: Megan gets on the phone with the sales rep and expresses concern in the marketing and client acquisition field of her business. She explains how she's tried building her business from scratch and how it's been a struggle for her to get her name out there, etc. The sales rep, Bauer, being the professional she is, asks Megan how this concern has impacted her business. She shares more details with Bauer. She then goes on to explain how she's tried *everything* out there and has yet to see massive success from any of her efforts.

Bauer goes ahead to pitch her solution, with Megan's permission and willingness to try something different. After a great consultation, Megan asks for some time to think things through and asks for a follow-up email on the product shown. They schedule a follow-up call and get off the phone from there.

The sign-up day comes, and Megan misses the call, so Bauer leaves a voicemail on her line. Weeks go by and Bauer goes back and forth with her until she finally agrees to schedule another call. When she gets on the line, Megan's nervousness screams louder than her words, and she says that she's already getting one to two clients with a company she's partnered up with a few months ago and wants to see how that works before she tries anything else.

Knowing what Megan is doing, Bauer asks her to reevaluate the importance of the concerns she shared on their initial call. She starts to sigh and admits how much of a burden and struggle it's been for her to get new clients in her doors, yada, yada, yada. In other words, Bauer gets her to *revisit* her pain points and helps her realize why they spoke to begin with.

After getting her past stage one, which is the purpose of the transaction, Bauer gets her talking about the numbers. (I mean, we gotta talk about the numbers, right?) She begins by talking about how she started with the other company (which she didn't mention before this call) and how she didn't have to pay for anything up front and all she had to do was blah, blah, blah. (It's irrelevant to the point in the call. None of the things she "just had to do" resulted in a positive ROI. In fact, it didn't result in any ROI.)

The longer Megan speaks, Bauer comes to see that she is an emotional buyer. She starts off by empathizing with Megan, and then explains how her story is all too common. Bauer then follows that by asking how much she is spending per month on her marketing efforts. Megan immediately goes into *defense mode* and says, "Nothing! See, that's the thing—I'm not spending a dime!"

Bauer takes a step back and asks her the question again. Megan can't understand why Bauer is pressing the point, so she starts to question the question itself.

Megan: *Well what do you mean by that?*

Bauer: *At the end of every business day/week/month/quarter, whatever timeline you have set for yourself to run the financials, how much money have you spent on this particular marketing company you've shared with me?*

Megan: *As I said, Bauer, I haven't spent a dime.*

Bauer: *Okay, so let's work backward here. How much does the average*
service at your business cost a customer?

Megan: *Well, depending on the service, roughly $50–$80.*

Bauer: *Okay, so let's meet in the middle here and say roughly $75. Does that sound about right to you?*

Megan: Yes. Yes, it does.

Bauer: Okay, so let's say you get a new customer in your doors from the marketing company, and he or she purchases a $75 service from you. How much of that $75 do you actually take home?

Megan: Hah! If I get lucky, maybe about $20? Maybe?

Bauer: So from every $75 service, you take home about $20 give or take.

Meaning you're losing about $55 per service. Would that be fair to say? *Megan:* Yes, sadly enough.

Bauer: Now, being that you're losing roughly $55 per service, you no longer have that $55, right?

Megan: Yes? So, what are you saying here? I mean, you know, I have to pay my staff, inventory, etc.

Bauer: Right, so what I'm getting at here is that—seeing that you're losing $55 on your average service, you're actually spending that same $55 every time an average $75 transaction processes through.

Megan: Okay?

Bauer: Now, how many of those clients would you say you get per week?

Megan: Gosh, maybe two?

Bauer: So on a weekly basis, you're cashing in about $40 for every service and spending $110 per week.

Crickets

Bauer: *Here, let me pull out my calculator. Please feel free to do the same. Being that you're getting roughly two clients per week, roughly eight per month from this marketing company, you are spending $110 per week, which equals a grand total of $440.*

More crickets

Bauer: *Now, you mentioned how you've been using this program for a few years now. Is that right?*

Megan: *I'm ashamed to say this, but yes.*

Bauer: *Oh goodness, and I hope you're not in a contract. Are you?*

Megan: *Oh gosh, no!*

You get the point, right? From there, Bauer would finish the full reverse ROI for Megan and own her business. That is how we win hearts and minds!

Customer's Side: So let's flip this around and look at it from the customer's standpoint. Megan has been experiencing multiple complications with her current marketing company. She feels she's tried everything with no results to show for it and it's gotten to the point where she's considered closing her business.

She comes across the company Bauer works for and, after seeing her full demonstration, Megan begins to feel a bit excited but also very nervous. She asks for a follow-up call; the closer she gets to that date, the more afraid she becomes. Unfortunately, she's feeding into her fear and allowing the negative memories of her past to define her reality. She decides not to speak to Bauer for a while. But finally, after a few emails from Bauer, Megan responds and agrees to schedule a follow-up call.

She goes into it thinking she'll just ask for another consultation, with no plans to purchase anything. After speaking to Bauer for a few minutes, though, she begins to trust that she truly cares about her business and is helping bring much needed clarity to her situation. After much back and forth, Megan finally agrees to give Bauer's company a shot and finds herself feeling excited about the new opportunity.

Bauer and Megan stay in touch, and after careful consideration and success, Megan decides to take advantage of the referral program. She gets multiple friends signed up and becomes a great advocate for the company. Bauer, on the other hand, uses this story whenever she encounters a similar prospect. What once scared Megan is now her go-to when it comes to any small business in need of a strong marketing team.

How would thinking long-term versus short-term have more significance to you?

CHAPTER 21: **TAP INTO YOUR INNER BAUER**

Reject ordinary, be legendary-Brad Lea

First, let's give a huge shout-out to all the badass women out there who have chosen a career in sales. Now, when many of us think sales, we think of sales*men*. Not sales*women*. So for all those women who have chosen to work against the stereotype and actually crush it in their field, here's a standing ovation for you. (I'm literally standing while writing this.)

As women in sales, we've all come across objections from male clients that don't ring true. Maybe he says he has to run things by his wife when at the start of the meeting he said he was the decision-maker. You have no choice but to call him out on it. Hey, you may even have to (politely) entertain his ego to bring in the deal.

We all know no male sales rep can say that to a male client, but a female can certainly get away with it. Now, of course, if we continue to *genuinely* and *respectfully* compliment here and there, the deal will soon be ours. I've been in countless situations where something I said that won the deal would burn the same deal if it came from a male sales rep.

So, listen up, ladies: We have a natural upper hand in sales, despite the old- school limiting beliefs. And don't think otherwise. Every time you look around and find yourself being the only female on the sales floor, own it because there's a reason it was designed that way. Next time you think sales is just a ‹guy thing› and there's no opportunity for women to capitalize, ask yourself:

How will the opportunities from my sales meetings today push me to tap into my inner Bauer?

CHAPTER 22: **A GIVE AND GET RELATIONSHIP**

Your skills have to be bigger than your fears-Grant Cardone

Let's talk about some raw cold calling objections. Below is a step-by-step cold call checklist I've used time and time again. From all my years in cold calling, I must say this has to be the most exciting part of the sale. Yes, closing someone down is also very fulfilling, but not as much as crushing a badass cold call, especially the tough cookies.

Before you make the call, look into your CRM history and refresh your memory on the last interaction the client had with your company. This step should take you less than 4 seconds to do, no more.

1. Stand up. You'll sound WAY more confident.

2. Go into the call with the following **action plan**:

You will get them on the phone (no matter what). Ask for the decision-maker, as if you know him/her.

Give enough value in a witty manner. (This will get them intrigued, and they'll be more likely to listen to what you have to say). Ask them questions (catered around your value prop) that will give you the answers and pain points you want to hear. (Smile!) Assume they are already in front of a computer. Say, "Do me a favor, John. Let's hop on [state the name of your site]." Make it a "we" thing so they don't feel alone in this decision.

Go in for your demo. Make it a natural and enjoyable conversation that you both value. Ask about budget, time, the decision-making process, what they're doing to [fill in the blank with your plan of attack regarding their pain points].

If John says he has to go, ask if a specific time later today will work to reschedule the call. (This will keep your product top of mind), Keeping a witty, short, and simple tone to your words is all that matters here. (Smile!)

Confirm the date and time. Explain the next steps. "When we get back on the phone today at 1 p.m., I will show you ... You mentioned how you had a hard time with ... (throw in a slight laugh). No worries at all. I have it noted here to show you our [mention your product or service tailored to their needs]."

Go silent. Wait for their response and excitement to settle in before you say anything else. Then say, "Perfect, now once we look over ... [again, only bring up relevant value props your company represents]. From there, we'll sign you up with a package you're most comfortable with. (Make sure they know they are buying and that you care about them and the decisions they make.) (Smile!)

Remember to keep your value props simple and short. You don't want to talk about yourself too much. Keep your dialogue focused on how your tools will help them. Get their input and agreement. (Smile!)

"Great! I look forward to learning more about your business and going over a program that I'm confident you'll love!" (MUST say this with enthusiasm. People buy from those with great energy.) Wait for yet another validation signal from them.

"Now, in the event that either of us has to reschedule, I will be sure to give you at least 24–48 hours' notice (depending on when the meeting was set for). I'd appreciate it if you can do the same." (They'll know your time is not something to play with. They will show up). Get their buy-in for the mutual plan. (Smile!) Thank them for their time.

Keep it formal here. Send them a calendar invite (even if it's for a 10- minute call). This gives the impression that you're busy and important. Remember that you want to respect their time and gain their respect. They will more likely respect your time if you set that boundary). (Smile!) Set up automatic text/email reminders.

3. Run the full demo.
Run the same or similar discovery scenario of questions. You want to know everything you need to know to close this deal. The strength of your discovery call determines the strength of your closing call. Recommend a package. (Smile!)

4. Process the transaction.

Use short, light tonality here. Make this sound like the easiest stage. Throw in some witty humor; keep them laughing and smiling. Get them excited. Throw in positive words to raise their energy as well. Share last steps moving forward. (Smile!)

5. Welcome them.

"Welcome to the [state your company's name] family!" and/or "I look forward to hearing about your success with us!" Give them your direct office and personal number, email, and best times to reach you. (This reassures them that you've taken care of them and will always be there to help them moving forward. You will seem like a real person they can call, text, or email when needed. This will make the sale easier to swallow once they get off the phone with you. Worst-case scenario, they get upset about something and you save your client and possibly get a referral out of them).

Words to use every time:

Let's: This takes pressure off the decision-maker and it makes it a "we" thing.

Excited: This brings positivity into the call and gets them energized.

Learn: This makes you sound like a student who's eager to learn about what they've done to get this far, intrigued about their future plans, and ready to help.

Success: They'll link your company with their success. **Family:** They will feel like they are part of a loving and caring community.

Most importantly, make sure you sound genuine when you use these words.

The moral of the story here is to find the value in the time you get. Whether it's a twenty-second call or a five-minute call, make the most of it. Make it more about them rather than about your commission check. Trust me, you'll get paid more in the long run. Be you, sound like you, and always smile, even if you have to fake it at first. With repetition, you'll naturally find yourself smiling more and more. This, of course, will result in an increase in sales which is more money in your pocket.

How will the give-and-get relationship skill contribute to your sales success today?

CHAPTER 23: **IN-FLUENCE**

The key to success is to focus our conscious mind on things we desire, not things we fear-Brian Tracy

Remember in a previous chapter how we were speaking about work ethic and how to be fulfilled in your sales career? Well, the message of this chapter goes hand in hand with that notion. Our influences not only make us who we are as people, they also shape who we become as sales professionals.

Take a step back and analyze who you are and what you engage in outside of work. Do you go home to arguments, toxicity, and drama, and then leave to go hang out with friends who can't seem to remember anything because of all the empty bottles lying around? Or do you leave the office to go to a safe, positive, drama-free home, and get started on your goals and fulfilling projects outside of work?

Read the list printed below and take a truthful look at your own life. Trust me, the goal behind this book is to help you sell and generate more for yourself, your family, and the brand you represent. This is your future we're talking about here. Check off any of the following that you engage in outside of work:

• drama

• peace

• arguments

- love
- slumping on the couch
- physical activity/exercise watching/listening to celebrity -drama
- listening to material that enhances your knowledge
- procrastinate as if you're getting paid for it
- get stuff done as if you're getting paid for it
- laugh at the idea of meditation meditate daily
- become "too tired" to work on yourself
- become addicted to bettering yourself

When we make the unconscious decision to allow our outside lives to negatively affect our work, and when we choose to live in what I like to call an unconscious and aimless state, we make the decision to let that affect our income flow.

So if what you bring in with you is good, by all means, bring it on in! But if we're talking about that family member or "friend" you can't stand, clear that story up inside your head before you walk in the next day. Focus on what you're at work to do. I'm assuming it's to create an abundant and prosperous bank account so it can support the lifestyle that you and your family desire.

The choices above are all yours. Ask yourself what kind of sales career you want. Work backward from there because if there's any gem I can drop in this chapter it'd be that your sales future is 100% determined by what you are doing right now. **The**

choices you make about your feelings, attitude, health, and emotional state all determine the money you make.

You want to be financially successful? Get your life in order, then work toward the money because your lack of money is not your employer's, manager's, or industry's fault. It's ... well, you get the point, right?!

How will you allow your outside influences to positively shape your performance tomorrow?

CHAPTER 24: **I AM A CHAMPION**

Each one, teach one-Denzel Washington

Take a step back and look at the people you deem successful. You'll notice a profound pattern. Whatever industry you focus on—sports, entertainment, self- development, movies, fashion, technology, transportation—they all have one thing in common: *constant growth*. Yes, the most successful people are passionate about what they do, and they all find fulfillment in their craft. Even beyond these values, successful people are always *rising*—always.

Look at any successful icon, and you'll notice they were striving for huge goals years before they found success. And today? They're still going! They're still growing and elevating their level of expertise, knowledge, and skill. And above all, they're embracing humility along the way.

Do you think these people were always successful? They just had it that easy? Of course not! What sets them apart from their peers? They ALL got comfortable with "failure." I used quotation marks there because I've consciously removed that word from my vocabulary, meaning I don't believe in its power or presence in my life.

By immersing myself in the teachings of Gary Vaynerchuk, Lewis Howes, Tony Robbins, Lisa Nichols, Oprah Winfrey, Grant

Cardone, Brad Lea, Bruce Lee, Michael Jordan, Bob Proctor, Will Smith, Kanye West, Eric Thomas, Denzel Washington, Mel Robbins, Vishen Lakhiani, Ryan Holiday and others like them, I've redirected my focus to a more abundant vocabulary. I've come to this simple understanding: It's not success versus failure. It's simply success *and* opportunity. Notice what I did there?

You see, opportunities for growth eventually lead to success. Even if you get down about something that didn't go your way, if you choose to see the good that came from it, you're golden. Now we don't need to be aware of the good that came from the opportunity at that specific moment in time. It can come later; and eventually, it will. The only thoughts we should focus on are the good vibes, thoughts, and feelings and reflect on how our actions build on that positive energy.

When you get to that point in your life where you find yourself continuously growing and reaching BIG, SCARY, JUICY goals, just do one thing: KEEP RISING! Soon enough, *this* will become your new norm. We're always students in life, and that will never change.

Just DECIDE

Make a choice. Just decide. What it's gonna be, who you're gonna be, how you're gonna do it. Just decide-Will Smith.

Decide that yesterday, last week, last month, or even last year was your worst sales production time. It is NOW that you

WILL do whatever it takes to master this beautiful survival skill called sales. Now is when you leave the lies and negative stories of your past behind. Now is when you will take control of your sales career, your finances, and the future that's waiting for you to put your foot down once and for all. I believe there are three types of people out there:

1. **Those who don't have goals.** These people are as average as they can be, and they're really good at complaining and "trying" to be successful, but they bring positive people down. *What do they do for a living?* you may ask. Oh, they complain for a living—no commission there. Bummer! Just wish them the best.

2. **People who have goals(phew!).** They achieve their goals and take care of their friends and family. They constantly move on to crush the next goal they have planned to achieve.

3. **Lastly, you have people on a WHOLE OTHER level.** These champions set goals, exceed them, and care for their friends and family. But they go one step further, constantly pursuing their mission, which is always out ahead of them, calling them forward. Well, that's until they've shared their knowledge, success, wealth, and blessing of an existence

with the rest of HUMANITY. Their goal is to achieve all of the above, turn anything they touch into gold, and serve a higher cause—to serve the human race.

What group are you in? Do you like to complain? Do you spout one excuse after another and attract drama wherever you go? Or are you focused on your goals and dreams so you can take care of those you love while being personally fulfilled? Are you driven by a higher cause, a higher purpose, a higher calling to serve something bigger than just your loved ones, hometown, and country?

Go ahead, be honest with yourself. If you're the first kind of person, don't get defensive; don't get mad. The good news is you can change! From there, take all the gems I've dropped in this book to turn your ENTIRE sales and financial success around. Whatever you do, do not—I repeat—do not judge or compare yourself to anyone in a lesser or higher group than you.

If you ranked at a higher level, have compassion, understanding, and love for those in the levels below you. Chances are you were once among them! So turn your life around by serving as a helping hand to anyone you can lift up. Inspire them. Let them grow from you and, of course, allow yourself to grow even further.

If you're thinking of people at a higher level than you, be inspired by them. Look up to them. Humbly reach out for guidance. Don't be afraid of "looking stupid" in front of them. Again, I put quotation marks around that phrase because as long as you know your why, mean well, and have a strong urge for growth, the opinions of others could mean nothing to you.

Run to the Finish Line

From the time I was a little girl, I told myself I would be one of those eighty-five-year-old super healthy ladies. Yet every time a marathon came up in the city I lived in, I'd pass it up for a half marathon or even a 10K race. Well, that all changed in early September 2017.

I heard about a local marathon that was taking place in January (four months away), and I signed up the same day. I began training religiously. I knew it was a great opportunity for me to grow mentally and physically. I thought, *What better way than to push myself to do something I've never done before?* I kid you not, when I say I was in tip-top shape mentally, physically, and emotionally. I was just on top of the world.

The race day came, and it was go time. I was excited as ever; nothing could bring me down. Everything went great ... until I hit the twenty-mile mark. As soon as I completed this mark, I started to feel intense pain in my right leg. It felt both on fire and completely numb at the same time; my leg was just *out of* service. So I thought, No worries, I only have 6.2 miles to go. I got this! I'm just going to walk for the next two miles and get back to running afterward.

Let's just say it didn't work out like that. As soon as Mile 22 came up, I tried to run. Instead, I stumbled on my remaining left leg for support. I figured it would be smarter to just wait it out and start back up at Mile 23. Well, Mile 23 came, and no matter how many positive affirmations I brainwashed my mind with, I physically couldn't get my right leg to run. Still, I wasn't ready to give up. That just wasn't an option for me.

Next thing you know I looked over to my right, and a man who had to be in his eighties breezed past me. What? Haha! I didn't care about winning this race. But I was not giving up! I was going to prove to myself that I could run those 26.2 miles.

I told myself, "Bauer, it doesn't matter who comes in first, second, or even in 200th place. It simply doesn't matter who beats you. But if there's anyone that does, it's not going to be that eighty-year-old that just breezed past you!"

From that second of realization to Mile 26.2, I did something I never thought possible. I not only got to the finish line before this man, but I finished the race by hopping on my left foot and dragging my right leg, ALL the way to the finish line. If there's anything I can take away from that experience, it's that there is no such thing as not being able to do something. No such thing.

Training for the marathon wasn't only about running a certain number of miles per week or knowing when or how to taper off; it was about *mental strength*. My thoughts drove me to that finish line. Had I relied on my physical abilities, I would not have made it.

Our thoughts run us. That's the ultimate truth. So if you're in a tough situation, make sure your main focus is on keeping a champion mindset because that is what leads you to that trophy.

How will you become your own champion today?

CHAPTER 25: **I AM LIMITLESS**

I am not your cup of tea, because I am limitless like you...-Rohit Choudray

Now that you've had some time to think, I want to circle back around to the idea of your omnipotent powers. Do you agree that we individually *create* our realities? As in, we decide if they are good, bad, fulfilling, or depriving? Can you see how we have the power to hold ourselves back? Do you agree that ONE person can change the world? (Shout-out to Big Sean.)

Can you accept that we all have omnipotent power within us to change a very negative situation into a drastically new, positive, and uplifting opportunity —not only for ourselves but for everyone involved?

We all have omnipotent powers over our own universe, reality, world— whatever title you want to attach to this existence we've been blessed with. We all individually created and made up what's in front of us! Whether or not you like what I have to say, you have to acknowledge that you brought this book into your life. And you decided to make this book out to be either the worst or best book you've ever touched or listened to. Am I right, or am I right?

Now that we've got that covered and you've admitted just like the rest of us you too are limitless, repeat after me: I AM LIMITLESS. I AM LIMITLESS. I AM LIMITLESS.

And what about this beautiful object we've given so much power? Yes, I'm talking about money—also known as moola, dough, or bread. Talk about a high- carb diet! Whatever form it takes, we all have an obsession, a love affair, with money. Anyone who disagrees and says, "Oh, money isn't everything," might as well be saying "Oh, blah, blah, blah."

*We **all** need money to survive.* We all have bills to pay and people or pets to take care of. We all have trips we want to take, things we want to buy for our homes, a new gadget we want to purchase. Not only do we all need money, but we *want it*. And, boy oh boy, the more the merrier! With that comes this **crucial** notion that we all have to admit: **Our relationship with money MUST improve.** The motive should be to find a way to attract it on a level like never before. For those out there who believe money is a bad thing, let's step outside for a moment of real talk.

There is nothing wrong with money. Money gives you a place to live, food to fuel your body, clothes on your back, and a fulfilling future to serve others.

Still not convinced? Still holding on to those limiting beliefs for dear life? I could be wrong here, but I promise to be honest with you. Chances are, your negative feelings about money arise from multiple sources:

1. Someone you know from the past all of a sudden got access to money and it changed them (for better or worse), but you just couldn't put your crap aside and be happy for them.

2. People with money intimidate you.

3. You get mad at yourself for not having it, so you don't want anyone else to have it either.

4. Your parents messed up and forced this limiting belief down your throat, and you messed up by believing and feeding into it. Hence, you keep rejecting the universe's offers of prosperity.

Here's the thing about money: it's not money that may remind of you something bad. It's most likely the person who misused the money that reinforced your negative beliefs. You see, just like anything else in the world, you have two choices. You can either use it for the better or misuse it, just for the heck of it.

There are people out there who make the mistake of letting the money get to their head, and they willfully abuse their power. These may even be the ones who "think" they can cover up their insecurities with the money they generate. Therefore, they blow it once it gets in their possession. If money could talk, it would say:

"You begged for me, and now that I'm here, you use me all up. But when I leave, you want me back?"

Then we have the true money manifesters and attractors. These men and women appreciate and use money in a positive and healthy manner. When it comes into their possession, they know just what they need and want to do with it. They respect their earned flow of income and do something positive with it. When they go shopping and see something that is above their budget, they don't say, "Oh, I can't afford that." Instead, they say, "That's not worth my $25," or "That's not within my desired budget." These folks act as if their money is ever- growing and constantly coming their way.

Keep in mind that when we change internally, everything and everyone around us will also change for the better.

What will you do today to tap into your intuition and make peace with money?

CHAPTER 26: **A 27-YEAR-OLD IS BORN**

Not one drop of my self-worth depends on your acceptance of me-Unknown

For as long as I can remember, I've always known one thing: I was going to be somebody. I was going to be someone who chose to find truth, embraced her areas of improvement, flipped her life around, and shared that same blessing with the human race in hopes of really signing off on a life well lived. I didn't know how or when it would all happen for me, but I sure knew I was capable. I knew that no one, and I mean no one, would hold me back from reaching my truest potential. That goes for all those I dearly love, have loved, and will yet love. I've decided:

I was born in that concentration camp in the Middle East, for a reason. I was put through those opportunities *by myself,* for a reason.

I was taught and pushed and pushed and pushed *by myself,* for a reason. I was thrown into training for that marathon *by myself,* for a reason.

I was forced to learn, hurt, and turn every bad into good *by myself,* for a reason.

That reason was so I can be right here, experiencing this precious moment with you. There was a reason behind all of those opportunities, and you best believe it was a monumental, precious, abundant, and positive one at that.

Selling my truth to myself was the most important sale I've made. Once I bought into the idea of believing in myself, supporting myself, finding my purpose in life, and really living it by pushing myself every single day on this planet, I've become the best version of Bauer time and time again. But don't worry, there's more of me to come.

I'd like to end this chapter by thanking you for wanting more out of yourself, your life, your sales career, your financial status, and your bright future. It's always been there waiting for you. And now you're on your way.   The importance of good energy is central. Remember, nobody knows you or what you're capable of better than you. Nobody knows your abilities more fully and intimately than you. Be your own leader. Value yourself. You become what you believe about yourself. The rest is the history you choose to create.

Act as if ...

Act as if today is your last day to smile.

Act as if today is your last day to not lose a thing.

Act as if today is your last day to take care of yourself.

Act as if today is your last day to show love to those closest to you.

Act as if today is your last day to do something that once scared you.

Act as if today is your last day to achieve that one goal you've been putting off.

Act as if today is your last day to go to bed fulfilled.

Act as if today is your last day to feel success being born inside of you.

Make today count. Make every day count. Do it today—not tomorrow, next week, or next month. NO. Start today. Lastly, I welcome you into this new world with arms open wide. This is a world where anything and everything good can be yours. Where greatness comes to those who are most deserving and who boldly believe they are worth having. Simply put, I welcome you into a world that's worth living.

What will you do today to live a more abundant, prosperous, and fulfilled life?

JOIN TODAY

Want to stay in the know and join other high performing entrepreneurs?!

Be sure to subscribe to my monthly newsletter over at www.bauerdoski.com. Once there, you'll find up to date blogs(ranging from how to master your business conversions to maintaining a wealth consciousness mindset), exclusive freebies, workbooks, and more.

After signing up, you'll be notified of any pending book and product releases, and be updated on content that may be helpful for your journey to success. You'll also be the first in line for exclusive promotions and future book giveaways. Looking forward to having you!

-Bauer

ABOUT THE AUTHOR

Bauer Doski is an Industrial Psychologist, Business Coach, Author, and blogger. Being the serial entrepreneur that she is, Bauer has created, sold, and rebuilt multiple ventures since her early twenties. She attributes much of her success to both her long-standing business acumen as well as her lifelong loved skill of persuasion.

Throughout her pursuits, Bauer has always focused on impactful work; work that held significant meaning in the lives of those she served in that it gave them the skills and resources to simultaneously improve themselves as well as their bank accounts. The business has always meant more to Bauer than just accumulating massive amounts of financial success and freedom, but being able to help fill the cup of others as she continues to let hers flow over; shed her light onto others. Only then is when she says is at most peace and knows all she is doing is going towards a great cause.

www.ingramcontent.com/pod-product-compliance
Lightning Source LLC
Chambersburg PA
CBHW071557200326
41519CB00021BB/6784